Leadership In The Heat of Battle

Lessons For True Leaders Inspired by Thomas "Stonewall" Jackson

by

Patrick B. Gillen

First published by AuthorHouse 04/08/04

ISBN: 1-4184-0843-3 (e-book)
ISBN: 1-4184-0842-5 (Paperback)

Library of Congress Control Number: 2004090062

Printed in the United States of America
Bloomington, IN

This book is printed on acid free paper.

"Are you in the heat of battle? Do you feel in your efforts to be successful in your current position that you have lost sight of what's important? Have you become so focused on a task that you have lost sight of your values, goals and the real meaning of your life? Do you want to be the leader you were meant to be? Maybe these lessons can help you.

By Patrick B. Gillen, BS, MA - Former Major-Select United States Air Force.

In The Heat of Battle

In the heat of battle, lies a place of supreme peace,

Hedged round by absolute trust in Almighty God.

There in complete calm come challenges seen clearly,

Plans are made quickly, unencumbered by doubt.

Sufficient strength is found, decisive action taken,

And victory firmly wrested from travail.

In that quiet bulwark amidst the tempest,

Is sublime safety and assurance,

That, "God's will be done."

No fear may enter there for,

Trust in His love

gives light and

life eternal.

PBG

DEDICATION

This book is dedicated to all leaders. Not managers, leaders. In this life we have far too many managers, and far too few leaders. It is for those who (as Ulysses S. Grant said of General Thomas) say, "Come", not "Go".

This book is dedicated to all those who serve others, putting their needs before self. It is for all those who love those they work with as a parent loves its child, and by so doing inspire them to do what was thought impossible. For those who serve as Christ did, and who love as Christ with, "greater love hath no man but to give his life for another."

This book is for all who give the irreplaceable gift of their time, talent, experience, and mentoring, without thought of self; because they believe in others. For all those who do their duty every day of their lives, for as Robert E. Lee said, "We cannot do more, and we should not wish to do less." This book is for all of those who wish and strive to be leaders such as these.

This book is dedicated to my team of men and women whom I am so very honored, proud, and thankful to know and be inspired by.

This book is only through the help Our God and Father who loves us and casts out all fear. My thanks to Him above all. He moved me to write this book for you.

And finally, my thanks to, and for, two good friends God gave me when I was in the heat of my battles to save lives and do the right thing as an officer in America's armed forces. He continues to help me with them in my business. Thank you Generals Robert E. Lee and Thomas "Stonewall" Jackson. Thank you for helping me see that in the heat of battle can be peace and safety, for our God is there too.

Table Of Contents

FOREWORD

From 1989-1999 I was an officer in the United States Air Force. There were many times I was in the difficult place of having to decide what was the right thing to do versus what was the politically popular thing to do.

It really wasn't much of an issue as I had been raised to believe that there was only one way to do things, the right way. To do what you believed was best and to give it your best.

Still I found myself often taking long walks with my dog, walking alone in cornfields and spouting out my frustration that if I as a Captain didn't have a problem seeing what was right, why did so many of my peers and superiors have such a tough time. My oldest daughter, Laura, who was 16 at the time used to walk with me and would often say, "Daddy you should go to the general and say that. You sound just like General Patton." I would laugh and say, "Honey if I expressed my opinion like that to the general I would be in the brig."

Of course we all face these same challenges. It doesn't matter what rank or position we hold. And we all have to fight that age old fight of deciding whether to do what's right or not.

As a nurse and an officer I faced life and death situations. I had to make decisions on my job that literally were life or death to someone's actual life or career. I couldn't wait all day or debate these issues. I had to form a decision based on the available facts and act on that decision immediately. There wasn't anyone I could talk to but God.

At about this time I began leading an informal class on leadership called, "The Call of Bugles." It was an informal lunch break meeting where great leaders were discussed after reading a book on that month's leader. A friend, Judy, recommended I read some books on the civil war. I was an avid reader about world war two and she felt that I would really enjoy reading about civil war leaders. I began with Robert E. Lee and became hopelessly addicted to civil war leaders. Lee, and later Jackson, became my mentors.

At my next assignment I became part of a formal leadership course. My wife and I began our own business and as I developed a team of other business associates I had to really hone my leadership skills. Before I had my training and rank and assigned position and the authority that came with that. Now I had to lead volunteers, so to speak. I had to gain the trust of individuals and get them to *choose* to follow me. So through reading, responsibility, and new experiences I began to explore what my personal beliefs on leadership and success are. What could I use to grow as a leader, and what could I pass on to others who wanted to be successful leaders.

At this same time I experienced the years 1992-2000 when it seemed that America's leaders had completely failed our people. I had survived the Vietnam years and Nixon years when more and more we began to lose faith in leaders who often told us untruths and who themselves seemed to become less and less ethical. Now I saw how the immorality of our leaders was demoralizing our nation and adversely effecting our youth. I saw a difference in many military leaders. The emphasis had been *their people*, now in the late nineties the emphasis was, *their pension*.

I came to believe that most of America's problems could be solved by inculcating in the leaders of tomorrow, yesterday's leadership values, skills, and techniques. To help bring our country back to the courage, devotion, and service before self, that characterized the signers of the Declaration of Independence.

I decided the best way to be a better leader was to read and learn from good leaders of the past, and to read what they read. In this journey I found that corruption, lies, and immorality

have always been a part of this nation of people, and of all people. It's no surprise there is good and bad in all people, no one is perfect. There is good and bad in all countries. They are all made up of people. Like people, countries can make mistakes. Like people, countries can learn from their mistakes and try and be better. In some ways we are better than our forefathers and mothers, in some ways worse. You see we all fight the same battles. Yet in the search I found two friends who inspired me and whose example guided me through my challenges. I also learned from many present day patriots and successful leaders about having balance in your life and how critically important this is. And now I felt a need to share my insights on leadership with others. I also decided that if I wanted to be successful as a leader I needed to compare my views with those of the wisest, most successful leader, and wealthiest man in the world, King Solomon.

ACKNOWLEDGEMENTS

There are so many people I need to thank and acknowledge. I cannot list them all, here are a few: Mrs. Irene Sagert an English teacher who believed in each of us; and was able to teach us English because we knew she cared. Mrs. Ellen Dennis, our high school librarian, who believed in me. I believe she was the first person who ever did. To Mr. William Daniels – "Pop", our high school chemistry teacher who helped us to feel that maybe we had value, because he invested his personal time with us.

To the many editors who mercilessly critiqued me in the past and helped really teach me to write. And, especially to the best editor of all, my wife, who has eagle eyes for typo's and loves me enough to tell me when something doesn't make sense. She has made me, and continues to make me, a better me in all areas of my life.

To my children, who believed in me when I was a young father, and who now that they are older, and know I am not even close to perfect, love me anyway. To my son Kurt who is the second greatest critic anyone could ask for, fast to see a weak area, and on target in advice.

To my mother and father, Edna and Aloysius Gillen, who I will see again someday. Thanks for always accepting me, loving me, for being there for 52 years, and when I had doubts and fears would say, "Don't worry. It will be all right. Trust in God. We'll pray for you. We love you son."

To men who have been my mentors in business: Bill Britt, Paul Miller,

Rocky Covington, Kevin Bell, Henry Skaggs, Alex Lind, John Cosgrove, Tom Tillman.

INTRODUCTION

SUCCESFUL TRAITS – ADVICE FROM A KING AND TWO GENERALS

If you have picked up this book and are looking it over then you are likely a leader who wants to be a better leader. In that case I am most honored you are holding this book in your hands and are considering using it as another tool to grow. Furthermore, you are most likely a leader who in leading has encountered demands, stresses, pressures, and who wants to become better able to deal with these.

It's most likely true that deep down you are hoping that this book will enable you to become such a good leader that you will then have less of these challenges. It is also probably true that, deeper down, you know that as you grow as a leader you won't have less stresses, you'll probably have more. But, you also know that through these struggles you will grow to be a leader that you will be proud of. I sincerely hope this book is of some value to you.

I believe we become leaders by wanting to help make this world a better place. We strive to become better leaders by reading, listening and observing others; by trying to adopt some of the traits of successful leaders into our own character; and finally by taking action, going out and using these traits, evaluating the results, and beginning again. It is a life long process, and if we really strive to grow, we will strain our physical, mental and spiritual muscles. We will fail and fall on our knees, get up, and seek and accept the help of better leaders. If we persevere, we may be blessed to become a person of influence who does in fact make this world a better place for others. If not by success, then by our example of striving for excellence.

And now a challenge. In striving to become leaders we are often exposed to things that may seem foreign to us at first. We encounter a new, different way of looking at something. If we have the courage to do that, we often find that, similar to cracking open a pecan, therein lies a good nourishing fruit, simply residing in a shell that initially appeared unattractive. This book may contain some thoughts or ideas you have not considered before. It is meant to help the leaders of today and tomorrow. I feel we are facing some real tough times currently. I know that all of us will experience challenging times. I believe that this world needs some good leaders; you may be one of them. I believe we can find some of the answers through looking at yesterdays leaders and what made them great.

I believe that if you really want to achieve success as a leader and do more than just survive struggles and trials, if you want to be victorious, to grow through it all, then you must find balance. You have to discover the core pillars of living that will provide a foundation so strong, so able to withstand anything, that you can then trust them and obtain that peace, assurance, confidence and calm that will enable you to see clearly, make wise decisions quickly, act courageously, and always be victorious, even in defeat.

I believe that one of these core pillars or legs that fosters success and achievement is faith in something bigger than ourselves. You've been warned. If this is a new area or not one you ventured into for a while, be willing to consider it. Practice the courage and objectivity a true leader needs. Continue on. If it is a familiar area, then welcome back. Thomas Jonathan Jackson believed,

"My opinion is, that everyone should honestly and fairly investigate the Bible; and if he can believe it to be the word of God, to follow its teachings." [1]

Robert E. Lee would have agreed. Many highly successful leaders in politics, the military, and business have found, and still find, it to be true.

After all Solomon the richest and wisest leader in history said, "The fear of the Lord is the beginning of knowledge." Proverbs 1:7.

James Robertson Jr. in the preface of his book, *Stonewall Jackson: The Man, The Soldier, The Legend.* Relates that almost in the center of Jackson's walnut bookcase are three works side by side. The Holy Bible; John Gibbon's, *The Artillerist's Manual*; and Phillip Bennet Power's, *"I Will.": Being the Determination of the Man of God.*

I feel that at the center of his being were three great drives, or priorities if you will. The desire to know, love and be with God; the desire to achieve honor for his family, success; and the desire to provide and share love of family.

I believe these same three priorities are the only way to achieve success as a person and as a leader. Like three legs of a stool they are all three important in obtaining a life of balance and success. All three are interdependent. Life consists in our keeping a balance among the three, and in placing the proper weight on each of the three, placing God first, family second, and one's calling third. If one puts too much emphasis on obtaining knowledge of God through immersing oneself in the Bible, one can become "so heavenly minded as to be no earthly good." We find God by looking not just in the Bible, but in ourselves, and others as well.

If we put too much emphasis on family, we can cut ourselves off from the source of strength and love and wisdom that we need to be of help to our family and others. Or, we can invest so much time in family that we are not able to accomplish anything for others. Finally, If we become a slave to our vocation, neglecting God and family, then we not only cut ourselves off from the source of knowledge and wisdom, but also the main reason for pursuing that calling.

So we seem to best succeed when we discover and maintain the proper balance. A relationship with God must consist also of loving self and others. It is in striving to do God's will in our laboring for and with others, that we meet, and serve, Christ in them.

It is in the context of family that we come to better understand and relate to God as Father, Son, and counselor/intercessor.

It is in the struggles of life and the challenges and trial found in our vocation, that we discover God's laws and how to apply them successfully. In helping our country, we help our family.

Returning to Thomas Jackson and his three pillars, or legs: 1) the desire to know, love and be with God; 2) the desire to provide and share love of family; 3) and the desire to achieve honor for his family, success in his calling- service to others.

In the life of Thomas Jonathon Jackson, God was at the center of his life, first and foremost, the chief pillar. He writes about his God constantly reassuring his sister that all will be well because of God. God was his anchor to keep the storms of ambition under control.

"In taking a retrospective view of my life, each year has opened…with increased promise…

I too have crosses, and am at times deeply afflicted…but I am improved by the ordeal…

By throwing myself upon the protection of him whose law book is the bible.

I would not part with this book for countless universes." [2]

Family, his second pillar, was the one joy in life that for so very long seemed to be denied him. Losing father and then mother at an early age, losing a brother, separated from his sister, losing his first wife and child; deprived of home and loved ones. Finally he achieves this goal in his wife Mary Anna. In his letters to his wife his priorities are reflected in what he wrote to her about. He writes about her, expressing his love for her and how much she means to him,

"In my daily walks I think of you. I love to stroll abroad after the labors of the day are over,

and indulge feelings of gratitude to God for all the sources of natural beauty with which

he has adorned the earth…As my mind dwells on you, I love to give it a devotional turn,

by thinking of you as a gift from our Heavenly Father." [3]

"Husbands love your wives even as Christ also loved the church and gave himself for it." Ephesians 5:25 [4]

Honor for his family I believe he saw as coming from knowledge and education; and ability gained as a student and practitioner of the art of arms. His drive to achieve honor for his family was obtainable through his vocation, his third pillar. In his letter he writes about the men he serves, the leaders he serves, the cause he serves. I find it insightful to note that nearly all officers of that time, as did many of our forefathers, signed their correspondence with, "Your humble servant,". I believe they saw their boss, their subordinates, their people, everyone, as those they served. Jackson writes,

"If I know myself, all I am and have is at the service of my country." [5]

As I read the life of Robert E. Lee I am struck by the fact that his whole life was one of striving to maintain balance in all his relationships, God, Family, others. I believe this is true for all of us who would lead. Lee saw the value of the Bible as an instruction manual for success,

"The Bible is the book of books." [6]

And,

"I prefer the Bible to any other book. There is enough in that to satisfy the most ardent thirst for knowledge; to open the way to true wisdom; and to teach the only road to salvation and eternal happiness. It is not above human comprehension, and is sufficient to satisfy all its desires." [7]

And again, as Jackson said,

"My opinion is, that everyone should honestly and fairly investigate the Bible;

and if he can believe it to be the word of God, to follow its teachings." [8]

Success Traits of King Solomon

I found in reading, and listening, to many successful leaders, that they often referred to Proverbs as the best book on business ever written. I began to reflect on the fact that in truth Solomon was one of the most successful leaders and wealthiest men in history. I decided to look for what he emphasized in his advice. I read the book of Proverbs and found that many themes were repeated over and over through out the book, in many cases word for word. I wrote these down and then for my own convenience categorized them into main points adding some insights from my experiences and studies as well.

Seek wisdom and understanding. Read the bible - especially proverbs, biographies, books on areas you want to improve in, and positive mental attitude books. The classics are great, remember you are what you,... READ.

Accept criticism, discipline and reproof. Listen to advice. You'll learn major lessons, much faster and less painfully. Seek wise counselors, the more, the better. Listen more than you talk, for you learn by listening, not talking. Gather the advice of numerous wise counselors and then use discernment and make *your* decision quickly; *and stick to it.*

Dream, have a vision, set goals. Set proper goals. Set BIG goals. Not goals of being rich, but perhaps goals of being wealthy, that is having money and time, to make a difference. Goals of helping tens of thousands of people. We have a BIG God. Dream big, plan big, achieve big.

Plan well. Be observant. Develop skills of observation and insight. Look ahead, count the costs, see the dangers and avoid them. Chart a course and press on.

Be humble. Avoid pride. Trust in God, not in self. Never praise yourself.

Be reverent. Know deep down that it was God who gave you life, your talents, and who sees your potential and believes in you. Respect Him, honor Him and give Him the credit and glory.

Choose your company wisely. Choose partners and employees, a team, who are faithful, trustworthy, and reliable. Don't strive for recognition or try to impress others. Associate with those who are successful and have Godly visions and values. The books we read, and the people we associate with do shape us.

Do what is right. Be fair and just. Walk righteously. Be blameless and obtain a good name, which is worth far more than wealth. A righteous man can always regain success if it is lost. But wealth without righteousness soon flees. You can make more money but you can't make more years of life, or easily correct a good reputation gone bad. Be gracious, defend and care for the weak, widow, and orphan. Help all you can. Many great men have shared that our lives are truly and best judged by what we have done for others, the positive difference we have made in this world.

Give 10% to God and 10% to others. Think of others and put them before yourself. That was how a sick, failing Rockefeller found happiness, success, health and long life.

Be an encourager of others. Always have a kind word. If you must criticize do it quickly, objectively, and in private. Then praise them for their many strengths. See people as God does. He sees their potential, not their weaknesses. Praise now, often, and specifically.

Be diligent. Focus on the work to be accomplished and do it well. Pray as though it all depended on God, and work as though it all depended on you. Those who focus on leisure starve.

Control your mouth. If you can't say something nice, don't speak.

Speak only to edify and help others. Be truthful, and pure, and brief. Speak little, listen at least twice as much. To be an excellent conversationalist ask questions to draw the other person out and get to know them; and forget all about yourself.

Control your temper. Ignore insults. Never act in haste. One slow to anger quiets contention. Again, if you can't say something good, don't say anything. He who avoids scorn has honor. When you speak, be quiet and in control of yourself, ponder what you will say first. Never reveal another person's secrets. Be a peace maker. Don't attack an opponent, simply present another way of looking at the situation.

Forgive and be merciful. Forgive 70x7 times, and be merciful.

Never borrow. Never get in debt. And if in debt, get out as quickly as possible. Budget for needs, and pay cash.

Never lend. Never charge interest if you do. Never take advantage of another's need. This is a means of losing friends and making enemies.

Trust in God. Turn it all over to Him, and leave it there. Know His will and act!

Be at peace. Focus on the positive and doing good. Don't envy, be jealous or worry. Unless you want to lose your health. Just focus on your duty; and let Him bless you for it.

In what follows I will share insights from my friend Thomas Jackson that have successfully helped me. And, I will try and discuss these insights in light of advice from King Solomon found in Proverbs. Come with me and see if you don't feel better about your leadership and yourself when we're done.

CHAPTER I.
A LEADER SEEKS WISDOM AND UNDERSTANDING

The person who would lead others needs knowledge in their area of endeavor, but ultimately a leader needs knowledge even more of human nature. He, or she, needs to know how people think, what makes them tick before he can motivate or inspire them.

Thomas Jonathan Jackson as a young man had nothing. He lost his father and then his mother at an early age and was farmed out to relatives. Though he had a place to stay and food and some caring and guidance, he had very little hope. He saw early on that education and knowledge was something he could control. When a local youth who had been accepted to West Point decided this was not for him and left, Jackson's influential uncle was able to get Thomas in as a replacement. He could increase his odds of succeeding at life and bringing back honor to the family name by getting a free education at West Point. As James Robertson says,

> *"He saw the military school as the one opportunity to improve his lot in life. Yet he was ill prepared for the classroom challenges of the academy. He struggled initially; he pursued studies falteringly but with an unbreakable determination expressed in one of his favorite maxims, 'You may be whatever you resolve to be.'"* [9]

It was said that he started at the bottom, 71st place, and graduated 17th, and that he did this by studying long hours. Fellow Cadet Jones stated of Jackson, that he…

"was always at his books and many times when others were asleep he was still at work." [10]

What did his efforts get him? A career in the military in artillery. Knowledge of an area of expertise, and likely some knowledge of human behavior and how to motivate others. A career when before, without education, he had little prospects of a future of any kind..

Later, when Jackson decide to separate from the military his knowledge enabled him to land a position at the Virginia Military Institute teaching artillery and natural philosophy. When a friend asked if he lacked confidence in attempting to teach he replied that,

"No; he expected to be able to study sufficiently in advance of his class; for one could always do what he willed to accomplish." [11]

One of my favorite quotes is, "Not all readers are leaders, but all leaders are readers." Or, "Today a reader, tomorrow a leader" by W. Fusselman. One of the very best ways to grow as a leader is to read; and I believe, the best reading is biographies. Did Jackson read?

According to James Robertson Jr.,

"…a favorite pastime: Anna reading aloud for them both." [12]

What did he read? Again in his book, *Stonewall Jackson The Man, The Soldier, The Legend.* Robertson tells us…

Jackson liked to read. His library was large and wide ranging. By 1861 he owned 122 volumes. History and biography dominated the collection. The twenty-six books in those subjects included classical studies of Xerxes, Mohammed, a history of the Jews, Plutarch's Lives, military treatises in Caesar, Washington, and Napoleon, national histories, plus popular biographies of Cromwell, Andrew Jackson, and Henry Clay. Religious commentaries were next in number with twenty-four. Specific subjects varied from exegeses on the gospels and John Bunyan's Pilgrim's Progress to self improvement guides for better morality. Eighteen volumes on science and mathematics reflected Jackson's academic responsibilities. The remaining books treated of health, gardening, travel, manners, and poetry." [13]

My father once told me that the best way to truly learn something is to teach to another. I agree, and I believe, that whatever we are given in this life that helps us, we owe it back to life to share that with others we meet in life.

Jackson began teaching a black Sunday school while living in Lexington. Despite being told that his running of a black Sunday school was against Virginia law he persisted and supported the school with tithes even throughout the war. I believe that Jackson had two reasons for teaching blacks in his town of Lexington to read the Bible. His desire that they know their God and the truths of the Bible; but I believe he also saw them as having no future, no prospects for success much like himself as an orphan boy. In teaching them to read he was giving the gift that had made such an impact in his life to others who had no hope without it.

His life while in Lexington was devoted to learning and teaching the art of war. On his own he acquired further knowledge studying the methods of Napoleon which he learned quite well. It was the self-training he put himself through, and the experience gained during the War with Mexico, and his reflecting on it, that led to his great success as a General in the war between the states. He took the initiative and sought the knowledge he needed . He became successful as a teacher and as a soldier.

But what about leadership? An officer needs to lead others, to do this he must understand human nature. And where did Jackson gain this more important knowledge of human nature? Some from his studies and training at West Point. Some undoubtedly from his own life experiences with others in war and peace.

When one becomes a member of the military he or she is immediately flung into an ocean of other individuals from all backgrounds. No matter how busy, friendships and associations form. In fact in the stress of learning a whole new way of living, individuals naturally gravitate to each other for support and understanding. Throughout one's military career when often restricted to base to perform one's duty the majority of the time, and especially when duty takes one away from one's own country, one's family is temporarily lost to him and one's military comrades truly become the only family one has during those times. These new associates soon become brothers. As a member of this family one encounters other individuals from all backgrounds. The country boy now finds these new "brothers", big city boys with unfamiliar accents. The Midwesterner finds himself rubbing elbows with southerners with rolling accents, and with New Englanders, and New Yorkers with nerve shattering accents from the borough. These brothers are of as great variety as crayons in a box. College graduates, common laborers, small town, big city, Midwest, New Yorkers, New Englanders, Southerners, and those from the old west and great northwest. Different accents, colors, faiths, morals, dreams; all thrown together and now brothers and sisters, members of a military family. You live and work together, and come to depend on each other. Deep down, by nature of your work, you come to realize one day that in fact your living at some point may depend on each other. All this diverse mass, striving together for, "God and

Country". One becomes more accepting, less judgmental, and learns from one another's experiences, successes and mistakes.

After a time like true family, there is a similarity, a resemblance. All look like members of the armed forces. Same hair cuts, same posture, same clothes are worn. But like family though there is a resemblance each is still a distinct person, a unique individual.

In addition through the military experience one comes to know oneself better. Will I do what I need to do under the stress of action? Will I fulfill my responsibility or let my team down? Will I be afraid, or calm? Will I think of myself or others? Will I wait for another to act, or will I go ahead and act when needed? Any failure stings and one quickly resolves to never repeat that action again. Any success brings with a new trust in oneself and confidence which leads to more striving to succeed. If a mistake made is not a fatal one, it too results in growth.

In addition to learning through one's own experiences, and those of his or her brothers, as one remains in the service, and acquires rank, and some authority over others, one also learns from these newer family members. Some of Jackson's learning no doubt came from his observing his cadets. Military officers learn about leadership through their studies and training, through their experiences. They are only able to lead others when they understand themselves and others, and what motivates and discourages them. Then they can communicate and motivate, inspire and lead. Life, work, and the Bible are the best textbooks for learning how to interact with others.

Lexington was a fairly cultured community, with two colleges one encountered people from all walks of life and with a bit of sophistication greater that a Western Virginia country boy was used to. His interactions with others in his community also taught Jackson a lot and he endeavored at this time to add to a book of Maxims he had begun writing while at West Point. His purpose seems to have been to become a better person and that he might be more successful in the social arena.

Jackson studied to become a better soldier and teacher. He also studied how to become better in his interactions with others. He applied himself to becoming a better friend, guest, listener, a better person in his community and society.

While in Mexico after the war he was exposed to people from a different culture. One can learn a great deal about himself and others when in a different culture. It offers an opportunity to become more understanding, to more objectively see other people's points of view, to appreciate them more, and to be more fair in our dealings with others. It appears that then is when he began to look at religion and what it might offer him.

He became more aware of a need to know God. We all at some point, need to answer the big questions of life. Is there a God? Is there something after this life? What will happen to me when I die? Where do those I love go when they die? Will I see them again? What is the truth? We realize we need answers to these questions, hopefully we seek to find these answers. Without the answers we will ever be less able to successfully cope with this life.

While at Fort Hamilton after the Mexican war three men, one a superior officer and the others ministers, talked with Jackson and led him to more closely consider religion. They helped direct him to find the answers to his questions. In 1849 he was baptized into the Episcopal church.

On arriving in Lexington he was exposed to a variety of Christian denominations:

...Presbyterians, Episcopalians, Wesleyan Methodists, and Baptists, he at first attended the public worship of all of their churches indiscriminately, listening with exemplary respect and attention....He now for the first time had a fair opportunity to observe the genius and working of

Presbyterianism under its better auspices; and he found its worship congenial to his principles, and desired to know more of its character. " [14]

In 1851 he was received as a professed member of that church. He soon after purchased a copy of the New Testament which became his family Bible. The first thing he read each day was the Bible and he underlined several passages. Robertson reveals, based on looking at Jackson's personal Bible, that Jackson's two favorite Bible verses appear to have been:

Revelation 21:4 "And God shall wipe away all tears from their eyes; and there shall be no more death, neither sorrow, nor crying, neither shall there be any more pain: for the former things are passed away." However the verse that most inspired him was Romans 8:28: "And we know that all things work together for good to them that love God, to them who are the called according to his purpose." [15]

So in addition to the study of books and the obtaining of knowledge through experiences Jackson also learned about human nature and life through the Bible.

"My opinion is, that every one should honestly and carefully investigate the Bible; and if he can believe it to be the word of God, to follow its teachings." [16]

Jackson discovered he had a need to grow in three areas of his life, 1) Vocation, service to others, 2) Interpersonal relations with others, 3) His relationship with God. Going from life to the Bible, and from the Bible to life, he found his way.

The Bible reveals much about human nature, how to succeed in business, and how to live a successful life. Proverbs was written by an extremely successful leader, and very wealthy man. If one desires wisdom then the answer is to: seek it, pray and ask for it, and listen to the counsel of the Lord and wise counselors. Or as King Solomon tells us in Proverbs…

"…incline thine ear unto wisdom, and apply thine heart to understanding." Proverbs 2:2 [17]

"Yea if thy criest after knowledge, and liftest up thy voice for understanding; if thy seekest her as silver, and searcheth for her as for hid treasures; then shalt thou understand the fear of the Lord, and find the knowledge of God. For the Lord giveth wisdom: out of his mouth cometh knowledge and understanding." Proverbs 2:3-6 [18]

"Wisdom is the principle thing; therefore get wisdom; and with all thy getting get understanding." Proverbs 4:7 [19]

"…with the well advised is wisdom." Proverbs 13:10 [20]

"Apply thine heart unto instruction, & thine ears to the words of knowledge." Proverbs 23:12 [21]

So we see this first characteristic of a leader, that of seeking knowledge and understanding, not simply residing in Thomas Jonathan Jackson but ever highly valued by him. Knowledge obtained by experiences, by study, and through the word of God. If then one seeks to be a successful leader, the pursuit of knowledge and understanding must become a way of life.

CHAPTER II.
A LEADER ACCEPTS DISCIPLINE AND REPROOF

Many years ago I thought I wanted to be a physician. In our small Midwestern town we had a physician who had been a family doctor for many years. He was known for his calm caring bedside manner and one day I decided I ought to talk with him. To make a proper decision I needed to now what it was really like to study, and become, and practice as a doctor. He asked me to come back to his small office. I remember it still, the smell of alcohol and phenol. His shelves were lined with reference books. His small desk was covered with papers and an ashtray full of cigarette butts. There he sat with tussled hair, his glasses hanging on his nose before blood shot eyes, a cigarette dangling from his lips, his tie neatly tied, his suspenders new. He talked a while and asked a few questions. He shared some of his experiences and then asked, "What in the world are you doing listening to an old fellow like me? Young people don't usually listen to older people and their advice?" Before I could think I said, "Well, I've learned I make less mistakes when I listen." Leo Cosgrove, "Doc" Cosgrove, was a good, kindly, doctor; and I feel a leader. He put others first and his example was not wasted on many in that town.

A leader listens to discipline and reproof for that reason. In order to make less mistakes. That way they achieve success and then preserve their gains without losing them.

Leadership is a combination of irony. To grow fast and successful one wishes to avoid making mistakes, yet it is in making mistakes too that we learn. Many successful men have shared with me that successful people are usually more successful than others because they failed more. That is they tried harder and inevitably made more mistakes along the way.

So it is by listening, especially to one who is correcting our mistakes, that we learn how to avoid future mistakes of the same kind and grow. But, it is also important who we listen to. Who we seek counsel from. Often in life it is from someone who has more experience than we do in the endeavor. Someone who has our own or the organization's best interests in mind. But in this day and time one must also acknowledge that there are some who may feel they would benefit from giving us bad advice, or from undermining our confidence and efforts. So it is also important who we associate with and take counsel from if we would be good leaders. Make sure your counselors are knowledgeable, successful, ethical, impartial, genuine; and who are unselfishly caring. Remember we become like those we associate with.

Seek *wise* counselors, the more the better.

"Where no counsel is, the people fall: but in the multitude of counselors there is safety." Proverbs 11:14 [22]

A true leader learns to rejoice in correction, for correction means growth as a leader. Marcus Aurelius had much to say on this topic.

" Suppose a man can convince me of error and bring home to me that I am mistaken in thought or act; I shall be glad to alter, for the truth is what I pursue, and no one was ever injured by the truth, whereas he is injured who continues in his own self-deception and ignorance." "Don't be disgusted, don't give up, don't be impatient if you do not carry out entirely conduct based in every detail upon right principles; but after a fall return again, and rejoice if most of your actions are worthier of human character. Love that to which you go back, and don't return to philosophy as to a schoolmaster, but as a man with sore eyes to the sponge and salve, as another to a poultice, another to a fomentation. For so you will show that to obey reason is no great matter but rather you will find rest in it." [23]

Another good thought is to remember,

"A winner knows how much he still has to learn, even when he is considered an expert by others; a loser wants to be considered an expert by others before he has learned enough to know how little he knows." Sydney Harris [24]

"Reproofs of instruction are a way of life." Proverbs 6:23 [25]

"Whoso loveth instruction, loveth knowledge: but he that hateth reproof is brutish." Proverbs 12:1 [26]

"The way of the fool is right in his own eyes: but he that hearkeneth unto counsel is wise." Proverbs 12:15 [27]

"A wise son heareth his father's instruction: but a scorner heareth not rebuke." Proverbs 13:1 [28]

"...with the well advised is wisdom." Proverbs 13:10 [29]

"Poverty and shame shall be to him that refuseth instruction: but he that regardeth reproof shall be honored." Proverbs 13:18 [30]

"He that walketh with wise men shall be wise: but a companion of fools shall be destroyed." Proverbs 13:20 [31]

"...he that hateth reproof shall die." Proverbs 15:8 [32]

"Without counsel purposes are disappointed: but in the multitude of counselors they are established." Proverbs 15:22 [33]

"The ear that heareth the reproof of life abideth among the wise." Proverbs 15:31 [34]

"He that refuseth instruction despitheth his own soul: but he that heareth reproof getteth understanding." Proverbs 15:32 [35]

What of Jackson? What are his thoughts on this subject? We know the great value he placed on gaining knowledge. We also know that he disciplined himself adhering to strict diet when he felt this dictated by health. If adherence to orders is an indication of how he felt about accepting discipline and reproof lets look at the importance Jackson placed on this.

One winter evening when snow covered the ground and it was bitter cold, the Superintendent of the Academy sent word to Jackson that he wanted to see him in his office. Jackson arrived precisely on time; he was asked to sit down. Then the superintendent remembering something he had to do, rose and told Jackson to remain seated until he returned. The worthy Superintendent meant to be gone only a few minutes but he got into conversation with some people and forgot all about Jackson. It was very late when he remembered him. He supposed Jackson had waited a reasonable time and gone home. But coming into his office next morning, he saw Jackson sitting bolt upright in the same chair as he had sat in the night before. Major Jackson interpreted the Superintendent's polite request that he remain seated for a few minutes, as a military order for him to remain there until he was relieved. Major Jackson never disobeyed an order. [36]

To Jackson, VMI was the Southern equivalent of West Point; as such, duty and orders were to be obeyed at all levels at all times. [37]

When he was asked to pray in church and failed miserably his pastor endeavored to spare him embarrassment by not calling on him. When Jackson met him on the street he asked if he were trying to spare him pain. When the pastor replied tactfully, "Yes", Jackson said,

My comfort or discomfort is not the question. If it is duty to lead in prayer, then I must persevere in it until I learn to do it aright." [38]

While on his honeymoon with his first wife Jackson announced that he was going to observe a Highland regiment perform its drill. When his wife and her sister objected because it was the Sabbath, Jackson at first rationalized it away and went. Later when they were together his wife again remonstrated with him for not honoring the Sabbath. After listening to her he said,

> *"Ellie: It is possible my premises are wrong. When I get home, I will go carefully over all this ground and decide this matter for myself." After making a thorough examination of the Sabbath and his actions, he concluded that he had been in error. Thereafter Jackson became unbendable in his spiritual observance of Sundays.* [39]

Jackson himself instructs us,

> *"Through life let your principle object be the discharge of duty: if anything conflicts with it, adhere to the former and sacrifice the later."* [40]

Dabney had this to say about his adherence to duty, to discipline.

> *One of the most marked traits of his religious character then, was conscientiousness. It ruled in every act and word; in things great, and things minute; in his social relations, and his most unrestrained remarks; in the regulation of his appetites; in observance of the courtesies of life; in the disposition of his time and money. Duty was with him the ever present and supreme sentiment."* [41]

Jackson seemed to prefer to discipline himself, so that another would not have to. He accepted advice and counsel, from those he met who were sincere and just. He then investigated their views and impartially decided what he should do. He then submitted himself to adhering to what he felt to be morally, ethically correct for him to do. Whether diet, finance, Christian duty, or whatever, he thoroughly studied the issue, drew his conclusions, developed a regimen to achieve the desired ends, and then rigidly adhered to it.

"Whoever loves discipline, loves knowledge." Proverbs 12:1 [42]

A final comment. Jackson throughout his military career as a general in the confederacy always consulted and listened to men who had thorough knowledge of the country they were fighting in. In this way he was able to make sound dispositions of his men and resources, and plan tactics to use terrain to allow him how best to attack his enemies. On one occasion he failed to do this, and that battle was at Seven Pines. History still condemns him for his failure to achieve much at this battle.

At Chancellorsville General Hooker's troops repeatedly warned him that Jackson was about to flank him and attack. Hooker refused to listen and was defeated by an inferior force of men.

Accepting reproof and discipline, employing self-discipline, adhering to duty, and choosing counselors who know what they are talking about, all appear to be quite important to a leader's success.

A final thought on discipline.

"My son, despise not the chastening [punishment, sharp criticism] of the Lord; neither be weary of his correction." Proverbs 3:11 [43]

"For whom the Lord loveth he correcteth; even as a father the son in whom he delighteth." Proverbs 3:12 [44]

I should interject, that it is possible, when disciplined by a human being, to be unjustly criticized. People are only human, and not all are good leaders, good at discipline. Can we learn something, benefit from, even from unjust, incorrect, criticism?

There have been times when I have been unjustly criticized and corrected. Occasions when I have been punished unjustly. Each of these experiences, though negative, actually proved a blessing in that they made me a better leader. I determined never to do the same to another. I did not want to be responsible for inflicting this kind of injustice and hurt on another. This resolve strengthen my self-control over my mouth, and always acted to stop me when about to judge and reflect on it more objectively. The result was I had far better interpersonal skills than many of my peers, offended others far less often, and was able to be a greater influence on my subordinates by my just actions.

As I grew older I learned something else. What would it feel like to have all of those I knew, all those I had devoted my life to helping, instead of thanking me instead unjustly accuse me, condemn me and hand me over to punishment? How would I feel if that happened? Then one day it dawned on me. Christ had done this for me. In a small way I now understood what Christ had suffered for me. Though completely innocent of any wrong, unlike myself, though God, He took on my crimes, sins, wrongs; and He underwent the accusations, injustice, and punishment for me. My relationship with Him has never been the same because now I know, and have felt, in a small measure, the price He paid for me, out of love.

The discipline you suffer, justly or unjustly, will make you a better person, and a better leader, one who understands what it is to be disciplined and so is just in disciplining others. Just as knowing the pain, and the consolation of Christ, helps you, so others perceiving that you have gone through what they are going through, and understand and care about them, this on-target consolation for them, has a major impact on them. And because you understand and are just, you will receive the trust and following of those others. The loyalty that ensues leads to your people following you, and to unity as an organization. This, team strength gained, is well worth the cost in emotional and spiritual pain.

CHAPTER III.

A LEADER USES DISCRETION – CHOOSES HIS TEAM AND ASSOCIATES WISELY

A leader chooses his team wisely. If one reads many books on leadership, one finds recurrent themes and principles. One of these principles is that who you will become is determined by the books you read and the people you associate with. A wealthy man was once asked what he would do if he lost all of his wealth. He replied that he would get a job as a waiter at a certain restaurant known for its being the haven for successful businessmen. He explained that by waiting on them he would obtain the information and guidance he would need to generate his wealth again.

When we read the biographies of great people we see traits they possessed. We see the things they did which resulted in success, and the things they did that resulted in problems. The entire book of Proverbs is King Solomon's observations on what traits or behaviors lead to success, peace, and happiness, and those which lead to failure, tragedy and loss. Plutarch does this same thing in his book, "Lives." We read these biographies and see what traits we have in common with the leader and think, "I have that trait!

I need to hone that trait or behavior. I need to develop that trait or behavior so I too can be successful." We see the positive trait and if we don't possess it we strive to develop it to increase our likelihood of achieving success.

We also come to see how other traits, bad habits, can lead to failure. We can then apply ourselves to ridding ourselves of these negative traits by self-discipline.

Some say we learn by two ways, knowledge and experience. We obtain knowledge through reading. Experience is the result of doing certain things and learning which are successful and which are harmful. We can learn from our own mistakes but it is even better to learn from others' mistakes. Solomon and Plutarch offer one means, another is observing life and events that occur around us.

We can further learn and grow through exposure to tapes, CD's, and books on leadership; through peers, and superiors. Many feel books are a very strong influence, stronger than tapes and CD's. A perhaps even greater influence is that which comes from experiences and associating with others.

We do become what we read and who we associate with. Jackson knew and appreciated this.

"A man is known by the company he keeps." [45]

Be cautious in your selection." [46]

"There is danger of catching habits of your associates." [47]

"Iron sharpens iron, so one man another." Proverbs 27:17 [48]

A wise man, a leader, chooses who he will trust with duties and responsibilities and information. He picks those who are trustworthy, reliable and faithful. Jackson shared,

> *"The Christian must carry his religion into everything Smith. Makes a man a better commander, a better shoemaker, a better tailor. Teaches him punctuality, fidelity…in the commander of an army, it calms his perplexities at a critical hour."* [49]

Jackson looked to ministers as sincere friends and spiritual counselors. [50]

In the Old Testament books of 1st and 2nd Samuel we see that Saul and David, the first two kings of Israel always sought to know God's will from his ministers before every battle. Jackson had a tendency to appoint ministers and theologians to his staff. He sought out men he knew he could trust and rely on, and who possessed talents he needed. He picked a non-military map maker, because he needed a good one and this one was good. He picked men he could rely on, believe in, and who he knew would work. It was said of Jackson,

"He never appointed a man to a responsible position without knowing all about him. He would make the most minute inquiries. Was he intelligent? Was he faithful? Was he industrious? Did he get up early? This was a great point with him. If a man was wanting in any of these qualifications, he would reject him, however highly recommended. No feeling of personal partiality, no feeling of friendship, was allowed to interfere with his duty. He felt that the interests at stake were too great to be sacrificed to favoritism or friendship. [51]

Jackson wrote in his book of maxims,

"Industry- Lose no time; be always employed in something useful; cut off all unnecessary actions." [52]

An unreliable messenger precipitates trouble, but a faithful envoy brings healing." Proverbs 13:17 [53]

"Every plan is confirmed by counsel, and thus by wise counsel you carry on war." Proverbs 20:18 [54]

A true leader then chooses a team that he or she can rely on. A group of experts in various areas, with different talents, that he can orchestrate into a successfully functioning group with a common goal. People he can trust to provide accurate information he needs in a timely manner. (Both Lee and Jackson greatly appreciated accurate timely information, they saw their cavalry units as their "eyes").

Each person has one or more gifts or talents. The wise leader finds these and allows the team member to use these to the fullest extent for the benefit of the entire team.

The wise leader delegates tasks to people he can trust knowing that they will be carried out and done correctly.

The one who would lead also counsels with other leaders and those wiser or more experienced than he or she is. He or she associates with those who possess the traits and characteristics he needs to be a successful leader. Knowing these will "rub off" through daily interactions.

He realizes he is effected by those he associates with and so he associates with those who are successful and fellowships with those who are Godly in their behavior.

A leader recognizes that he too will affect, or influence, those that associate with him. He must be a person, that when emulated, causes others to succeed. Those positive traits he has will be picked up by his team, so it is good to develop and be an example of these. Unfortunately, the negative traits will be picked up as well and mistakes and headaches multiplied. So it's best he eliminates these from his make up through self-discipline.

Finally, the successful leader comes to see that to be worthy of trust a leader realizes he must be himself, not striving to impress and garner recognition falsely. As Jackson said,

"A man of words and not of deeds is like a garden full of weeds." [55]

To truly be influential and to make a lasting impression on others, to make a difference, one must be a truly good, righteous, person. Not just appear to be that.

He talked of what he considered the right sort of man. "One always striving to do his duty and never satisfied if anything better can be done." [56]

He also realizes his people will be what he is, so he strives to always be a good example.

"...within the past years, I have endeavored to live more nearly unto God. And now nothing earthly could induce me to return to the world again... For my part I am willing to go hence when it shall be his great will to terminate my earthly career...Rather than violate the known will of God, I would forfeit my life. It may seen strange to you, but nevertheless such a resolution I have taken, and I will by it abide." [57]

One leadership author I know talks about being transparent. When someone reveals their true selves to another, when they are said to be, "transparent"; then that other really knows them. Only in this way can they deepen the bond with the other, strengthen the relationship.

He frequently prayed in the sight of his troops, serving as an example and an encouragement. When his troops had safely passed over a river after a battle, "With raised hands he looked upward, closed his eyes, and engaged in silent prayer for an unusually long period. [58]

Having developed many positive traits his transparency resulted in his men embracing his leadership and example.

To most of the men who were his troops Stonewall Jackson was…"greatest and noblest in that he was good, and…gave his talent and his life to a cause that, as before the God he so devotedly served, he deemed right and good." [59]

In all fairness Jackson had one fault. He tended to trust no one with information about his plans. He erred on the side of having too much discretion and trusting no one to perfectly keep a secret. So much so that his officers had no idea where they were going or why. Lee tried to warn him that this resulted in lack of coordination and problems, but he never seemed to learn this as well as might be expected, although he did appear to improve somewhat.

The above illustration makes a good point. When using discretion in communicating information, there is no set rule. How much should the leader tell? One might err by being too secretive, or not secretive enough. Many leaders, to include Solomon, warn about revealing too much to others.

"A man of insight conceals his knowledge." Proverbs 12:23 [60]

"He who guards his mouth controls himself, but he who opens wide his lips comes to ruin." Proverbs 13:3 [61]

Your people have to know what to do and perhaps why, but competitors and opponents can and will use any information they obtain against you.

Consider these examples and others through reading and association, and try and learn from the errors, the right amount of discretion for each occasion.

CHAPTER IV.
A LEADER PLANS WELL

I believe it was John Maxwell who said that a leader looks ahead at where he is going and what obstacles lie ahead, and tries to chart a course that will navigate him successfully to his destination.

A leader must do four things then in order to be successful in his or her endeavors:

1) The leader must know where he or she is going, that is, the leader must have a goal.

2) The leader must look ahead and gather all the data possible. The leader must assess what he or she will have to overcome to achieve that goal.

3) The leader must plan how to overcome these obstacles and achieve the goal.

4) The leader must act. They must cast the dye, commit to it, believe and put all they have into it. With charts, crew, and supplies in hand

he or she must BEGIN, the journey.

Jackson was a military leader, but let us not lose sight of the fact that he was also a teacher, a spouse, a member of Lexington society, and a church member. In each of these roles he had duties, goals, and plans to succeed in all three areas of his life. He planned to succeed in vocation, in his relationship with his spouse, and in his relationship with his God. He strove to keep all three in balance.

Perhaps you are not a military leader. But you have goals to succeed in all areas of your life. You have a need to grow and equally strengthen all areas of your life, to achieve a balanced, prosperous life. Like Jackson we can apply the four parts of making our journey towards our goals.

1) To pick a goal, set a destination. First we need to decide where we are going.

Jackson decided he wanted to gain fame in his vocation, to be successful as a master of the art of warfare. Initially his goal was to gain recognition as an artillery officer. Later his goal changed somewhat to becoming a teacher of artillery and natural philosophy, or Physics, at the Virginia Military Institute. Finally he obtained lasting fame as a victorious general in the armed forces of his country. Throughout his life he strove towards these goals by studying, by mastering the knowledge, and later successfully applying what he learned.

West Point was the greatest challenge of Jackson's formative years. He saw the military school as the one opportunity to improve his lot in life. Yet he was ill prepared for the classroom challenges of the academy. He struggled initially; he pursued studies falteringly but with an unbreakable determination expressed in one of his favorite axioms: "You may be whatever you resolve to be." [62]

First classman Ulysses S. Grant is supposed to have remarked at one point during the year that Jackson "was the most honest human being I ever knew-painfully conscientious, very slow in acquiring information, but a hard, incessant student." [63]

Jackson's wife shares with us,

He had a library, which though small, was select, composed chiefly of scientific, historical, and religious books, with some of a lighter character, and some in Spanish and French. Nearly all of them were full of his pencil marks, made with a view to future reference. [64]

Cadet Jones knew that his friend "was always at his books and many times when others were asleep he was still at work." [65]

So we see that he always strove to improve, and to forge ahead to obtain goals.

In his relationship with God he strove to be the best Christian he could be. Once aware of the need to make a decision in this area he listened to the counsel of older officers, more experienced in this area than he. He interviewed various ministers and attended various churches.

Colonel Frank Taylor...his first spiritual guide. His instruction and prayers had produced so much effect as to awaken an abiding anxiety and spirit of inquiry in Jackson's mind...He acknowledged his former practical neglect of this transcendent subject, and deplored the vagueness of his religious knowledge...He resolved to make the Bible his study...[66]

He at first attended the public worship of all of their churches indiscriminately...[67]

Once he found the church that best fit his beliefs he joined and studied its catechism.

He now, for the first time, had a fair opportunity to observe the genius and working of Presbyterianism...he desired to know more... The result of his inquiries was...he was received, by profession of faith, as a member of that church.[68]

He felt it a duty to adopt a strict moral code of conduct in order to live his religion every waking hour of the day. A starting point was systematic reading of the Bible and religious books.[69]

He strove to learn as much as he could about being a good man, a man of faith. And, he strove to have the relationship with God he felt we are called to have.

He strove to be successful socially. He studied books on etiquette and by studying, observation, and trial and error he became successful in

32

developing and maintaining relationships.

During his time at West Point he began to compose a book of Maxims.

They were simply intended to assist a timid, socially untutored young man in mastering the challenges of daily life in a learned society. [70]

Later he strove to be successful in having a family, in obtaining a wife and home. He writes,

I hope we shall be able to call some house our home…I shall never be content until I am at the head of an establishment in which my friends can feel at home in Lexington. I have taken the first important step by securing a wife capable of making a happy home, and the next thing is to give her an opportunity. [71]

Whatever it is we wish to succeed in and master, we must first decide what field, in what way. We must set the goal and then set a date to achieve it by. There was a famous study done at one of the major universities in the 20th century. They researched what happened to people who wrote down their goals. They found that the 20% of the classes that did acquired 80% of the wealth created by that class. They found that the 80% who did not write down their goals acquired the remaining 20% of the wealth created/ acquired. There is also the story of the movie star who when discouraged would sit on one of the hills in California and take out a check he had written himself for over one million dollars. He became successful and was paid for making his first movie the amount on the check he had written years before, AND, the date was only off a few days!

Having determined a goal and set a date to achieve it, we must next apply ourselves to master the knowledge through the study of books, counseling with instructors and mentors, applying what we've learned, practicing it and acquiring experience in the field.

2)   Observe the obstacles, and assess what has to be faced. We need to look ahead and discover what we will have to overcome.

As a general over an army Jackson gathered data he needed through the cavalry, mapmakers, and personal reconnaissance.

Shortly after these orders went forth, Jackson decided to reconnoiter personally. He galloped towards the Potomac. By the time Hill arrived with his lead brigade, Jackson not only knew the situation but had developed his strategy. [72]

In this way he was able to see the entire situation, to observe and take in the terrain and see where the strengths and weaknesses lie and how and where to obtain a position of strength to attack or defend. We ever need to look ahead and realistically assess what obstacles we need to overcome.

3) Plan. We need to plan how to overcome the obstacles and be victorious in our efforts.

Jackson, having weighed the odds, against him (often when as much as 2:1 or 10:1) looked for an advantage until he found it. As Jackson himself stated,

> *"Always mystify, mislead, and surprise the enemy, if possible; and when you strike and overcome him, never let up in the pursuit as long as your men have strength to follow; for an enemy routed, if hotly pursued, can then be destroyed by half their number. The other rule is, never fight against heavy odds, if by any possible maneuvering you can hurl your own force on only a part, and that the weakest part, of your enemy and crush it. Such tactics will win every time, and a small army may thus destroy a large one in detail, and repeated victory will make it invincible."* [73]

In warfare it is critically important to be able to put yourself in another's place and figure out what he would do. Then you can plan what you will do. Lieutenant Colonel GFR Henderson felt that both Jackson and Lee had this ability. [74]

Whether directing our efforts against opponents, or competitors, or obstacles, we need to include in our plans how we will overcome them.

4) Act. In order to complete our journey, attain our goal, reach our destination, we must first set out. Deciding on a goal is important.

Realistically appraising the pro's and con's is essential. Planning for every contingency is vital. But if we don't at some point set out, act, charge forward, set sail, all is for naught. We will never achieve anything.

Jackson saw this.

I expect to be able to study sufficiently in advance of my classes; for one can always do what he wills to accomplish. [75]

It is no time, when the tide of victory bears him forward, for a general to take counsel of his fears. [76]

Even when obstacles or opponents appear formidable, put your plans into action. Jackson tells us in any undertaking to employ industry.

"Industry-lose not time; be always employed in something useful; cut off all unnecessary actions." [77]

As Henderson says,

A time comes in all protracted operations when the nervous energy of the best troops becomes exhausted, when the most daring shrink from further sacrifice, when the desire of self-preservation infects the stoutest veterans, and the will of the mass opposes a tacit resistance to all further effort. "Then", says Clauswitz, "the spark in the breast of the commander must rekindle hope in the hearts of the men, and so long as he is equal to this he remains their master. When his influence ceases and his own spirit is no longer enough to revive the spirit of others, the masses, drawing him with them, sink into that lower region of animal nature which recoils from danger and knows not shame. Such are the obstacles which the brain and courage of the military commander must overcome if he is to make his name illustrious." [78]

Act! The leader must find the inner strength to act and to motivate all those around him to action. Jackson, addressing the young men of VMI

when war was eminent said,

"Military men when they make speeches, should say but a few words, and
speak them to the point. I admire young gentlemen, the spirit you have
shown in rushing to the defense of your comrades; but I must commend
you particularly for the readiness which with you have listened to the
counsel and obeyed the orders of your superior officers. The time may be
near at hand when your state will need your services, and if that time does
come, then draw your swords and throw away your scabbards." [79]

True leaders don't just talk the talk, to achieve success they must walk

the walk as well.

Set a goal. Assess the costs and challenges. Plan, taking advantage of

strengths. Act.

When I was in a flying squadron as a Captain I set three goals for that

tour of duty. 1. To obtain senior flight wings rather than regular wings. 2.

To become a major. 3. To obtain a commission in the Regular Air Force. I

studied hard, excelled in each area. I got a duty that demanded I fly extra

and stay a year longer than normal in that assignment. I applied myself

at each level and did more than was expected of me. My last few months

there I obtained my senior flight wings and commission. On arriving at

my next assignment I found the recommendation written for me at my last

assignment got me promoted to major.

1) Set your goals and assign dates. 2) Look ahead and assess risks, challenges, and obstacles. 3) Develop plans to overcome these and to obtain your goals. 4) ACT. Act wisely, diligently, wholeheartedly. Press on when tired and achieve your desires. And, if you are a leader, lead your people to act. You set out, then turn and say, "Come, follow me, we can do it."

CHAPTER V.

A LEADER IS NOT WISE IN HIS OWN EYES; BUT TRUSTS IN GOD ALONE

In the last chapter we saw that a leader must have a goal, gather information, develop a plan and act. To get the best results the goal must be one that matters to him. The, "WHY?" must invoke passion and the commitment necessary to result in success. The information must be timely and accurate. The plan must be the best possible way to ensure the desired results. The action must be the right type, at the right time, and coordinated. Efforts must be unified, actors committed. All this is necessary if we would maximize the chances for success.

A leader should desire the best information possible to enable him or her to make the best decision that will benefit the people served. The leader becomes one worthy of trust and increases others confidence in him and allegiance through victories. When people know what they are doing is going to result in successfully overcoming a challenge, they become more passionate about doing it. Not too many of us will put our all into a project likely to fail. Most of us will put in not only what is required, but more when we believe we will be victorious.

The more a leader is able to achieve results beneficial to those served, the more others will follow and obey his suggestions and commands, no matter what. So, good information and good advice, increase the chances for a better decision and outcome. Success then obtained leads to confidence and trust in ones followers, which in turn lead to allegiance and unquestioned following. The end result is more unified action, and all this increases the likelihood for success. More success leads to more confidence and greater allegiance and so a momentum is gained that pushes the leader to the top.

It is crucial to the leader to be able to put complete faith in the information, make the best decision possible, and act with complete confidence. To be able to consider all the information, and weigh all the options and decide on the best way to accomplish what is desired, a leader must be objective. He or she cannot afford to be overconfident, for that leads to failure.

In order to put his, or her, entire self in back of the plan, decision, and action, a leader must be convinced that it is the best way, the very best course to take. Especially when the stakes are high. Jackson was no different than any other leader in this. He always sought to obtain the best information and advice, and then deciding on the best course, he acted on it with his all.

A leader who is not wise in his own eyes will more readily accept counsel from others in order to arrive at the best decision. They will gather all the information and advice they can from others whom they respect. They may not always like all of those others. Lincoln had a group of men he highly respected but many were enemies of his politically. When warned about this by his aides he said that it didn't matter, what mattered was their talents and what they contributed for the nation. He respected their skills and opinions, what they thought about him did not matter. Robert E. Lee once recommended a man for a position. He was told that man had said unkind things about him. Lee replied that did not matter, he was asked his opinion of that man for a position, and he gave that opinion. The benefit recognized by the people was what mattered. This humility we will look at again in chapter seven.

We have seen that leaders acquire the wisdom they need through their own study and experiences, through their mentors and counselors. They get the information and advice they need from peers and team members they trust and respect. Once they obtain all the information they need, or at least as much as possible, they make a decision and they act. Unless they make a decision and act, all is for naught. I can learn what is the perfect or best stove and fire wood. I can purchase the perfect stove, locate and obtain the best firewood, but unless I decide that all is ready and decide to start the fire. Unless I strike the match and apply the flame, no fire results, no heat, I stay cold. A leader obtains the best information, and then makes a decision.

The decision calls forth action and the action results in success or failure. But, the repercussions of the decision and action can be formidable. As the decision maker perhaps a large sum of money is at stake. Perhaps the future of our business or even our own career may be at stake. If we are a leader, the careers and even lives of our people may be at stake. The anxiety resulting when we view the magnitude of the effect on ourselves, those we lead and those we serve can nearly immobilize us. The judgment is ours, yet the magnitude of the consequences can lock us into indecision. How can we obtain that certainty we need to not only proceed, but to confidently steam ahead?

There is one source of additional counsel and guidance we have not yet addressed and that source is God. Those who believe in God believe that he is more knowledgeable. Many believe that he hears our prayers and petitions for help and guidance. In addition many believe that He cares about us.

If He is all knowing, all wise, and cares about us, it appears to then follow that we would seek His advice and guidance, especially when stakes are high. It also follows that if we know Him, and can then fully trust in Him, then and only then may we precede in perfect confidence; calm, unafraid, and assured of the best outcome.

Thomas Jonathan Jackson was such a person and this was one of his main characteristics. As his aide, James Power Smith said,

"The religion of Jackson was the man himself. It was not only that he was a religious man, but that he was that rare man among men to whom religion was everlasting... The religion of Stonewall Jackson will be the chief and the most effective way into the secret spring of the character and career of this strong man." [80]

Jackson's faith enabled him to make sense of life.

"Buoyed by faith. Jackson came to understand that his youth, and the deaths of his parents, siblings, first wife, and first two children were all part of a divine purpose. Turning to God because he had no where else to go, Jackson fervently absorbed the Biblical assurance that all things work together for good to them that love God." [81]

That kind of faith enables us to trust in God, and to go forward and act.

When we look for answers in life, we study and listen to others more experienced, and usually find our answer. Once believing in God's existence, and then embarking on a path of study, prayers and seeking, one finds Him. I have found it only necessary to seek and do my part, and then be still and listen, to hear that which I had not been able to, to know and experience that which I had not.

Jackson sought his God and found Him. He found him to be all that he was told and believed. He found he could trust Him completely.

Harvey Hill, also a man of great faith, said,

"The striking characteristic of his mind [became] his profound reverence for divine… authority. I never knew anyone whose reverence for divine authority was so all pervading, and who felt so completely his entire dependence upon God." [82]

I believe Jackson perhaps is best summed up by this passage from the Bible…

Happy is he that hath the God of Jacob for his help, whose hope is in the Lord his God. Psalm 146:5 [83]

A cadet who knew Jackson said,

"He laid every plan, purpose, and desire before his Great Master, implored His direction, and when assured what the will of God was, he never deviated one hair's breadth from the path of duty." [84]

This in fact seems confirmed by Jackson himself who said,

"We should always seek by prayer to be taught our duty." JIRp[85]

We seek to know what to do, how to apply our lives, "What is it God wills for me to do?" He looked to God and the Bible for guidance in all things.

> *"At a council of war one night, Jackson had listened very attentively to the views of his subordinates, and asked until the next morning to present his own. As they came away A.P. Hill laughingly said to Ewell, 'Well I suppose Jackson wants time to pray over it.' Having occasion to return soon afterwards to get his sword which he had forgotten, Ewell found Jackson on his knees, and heard his ejaculatory prayers for God's guidance in the perplexing movements then before them, by which he was so deeply impressed, and by Jackson's general religious character, that he said, 'If that is religion, I must have it.' and in making a profession of faith not long after, he attributed it to the influence of General Jackson's example."* [86]

Once we know His will, then we search how to accomplish it. We seek His guidance in planning and His blessing on our actions.

> *He asked Captain James Power Smith, "Can you tell me where the Bible gives generals a model for their official reports of battles?" Smith answered that he had never consulted Holy Writ to find examples of battle reports. Jackson said, "Nevertheless there are such: and excellent models too. Look, for instance, at the narrative of Joshua's battle with the Amelikites: there you have one. It had clearness, brevity, fairness, modesty; and it traces the victory to its right source, the blessing of God."* [87]

As we experience His guidance, we come to seek it more and more. We seem to come to know His will, His voice, more easily and more clearly.

Robertson in his book states of Jackson,

> *"Jackson resented praise, Glory for his achievements belonged to God."* [88]

> *"Victories came solely from God, who was alone entitled to the credit. Early ambition, as well as an excess of love between all humans save inside families, was wrong."* [89]

45

Thus always, whatever his army achieved, his modesty lead him to ascribe it to his brave men, feeling himself to be but an humble instrument in the hand of God. [90]

Trust in the Lord with all thine heart; and lean not unto thine own understanding. In all thy ways acknowledge him, and he shall direct thy paths. Proverbs 3:5-6 [91]

Obviously, if our efforts are guided and blessed by God, and our success is a result of this, then we owe Him the credit, the praise and the glory.

Jackson said,

"Duty is ours; the consequences are God's." [92]

As he believed that God alone would decide the outcome he greatly valued prayer; both his own and the prayers of others for his army.

"All glory be to God for his unnumbered blessings...Let us all unite more earnestly in imploring God's aid in fighting our battles for us. The thought that there are so many of God's people praying for his blessing upon the army, which in his providence, is with me, greatly strengthens me. If God be for us, who can be against us? That he will still be with us, and give us victory after victory, until our independence shall be established, and that he will make our nation that people whose God is the Lord, is my earnest and oft repeated prayer." [93]

This faith in God gave him confidence and strength even when his men and resources were not all that he could desire.

"He never balked at battle because his subordinates were inexperienced. His reliance was primarily on discipline, upon himself, and upon God, not upon the eminence of the officers." [94]

Put not your trust in princes, nor in the son of man, in whom there is no help. Psalm 146:3 [95]

This observation from the Bible,

"It is better to trust in the Lord than to put confidence in man. It is better to trust in God than to put confidence in princes. Psalm 118:8-9 [96]

is echoed by Jackson,

"I have almost lost confidence in man. When I thought I had found just such a man as I needed, and was about to rest satisfied in him, I found something lacking in him. But I suppose it is to teach me to put my trust only in God." [97]

Put not your trust in princes, nor in the son of man, in whom there is no help. Psalm 146:3 [98]

Some trust in chariots, and some in horses: but we will remember the name of the Lord our God. Psalm 20:7 [99]

When one considers the overwhelming odds which he so often faced in battle how could he have made decisions and committed his men with such confidence? As I read his words and study his life I can almost hear him quote these scriptures…

Commit thy way to the Lord; trust also in him: and he shall bring it to pass. Psalm 37:5 [100]

Blessed is that man that maketh the Lord his trust and respecteth not the proud, nor such as turn aside to lies. Psalm 40:4 [101]

For I will not trust in my bow, neither shall my sword save me. Psalm 44:6 [102]

But I will trust in thee. Psalm 55:23 [103]

What time I am afraid, I will trust in thee. In God I will praise his word, in God I have put my trust; I will not fear what flesh can do unto me. Psalm 56:3-4 [104]

Ye that fear the lord, trust in the Lord: he is their help and their shield. Psalm 115:11 [105]

In letters to his wife Jackson writes,

"What a consoling thought it is, to know that we may, with perfect confidence, commit all our friends in Jesus to the care of our Heavenly father, with an assurance that all should be well with them." RLDp121 [106]

Happy is he that hath the God of Jacob for his help, whose hope is in the Lord his God: Psalm 146:5 [107]

He interceded for all those in his care…

Recognizing the sovereignty of the Lord of Hosts, he interceded for his veterans, that "the Almighty would cover them with his feathers, and that his truth might be their shield and buckler." [108]

…it was observed that he was much in prayer, but this was his custom previous to every battle. Even upon the field he was often seen to lift his eyes and raise his right arm as if in earnest prayer, and sometimes it seemed that while his soul was thus lifted up in supplication, the Lord of hosts heard and answered, giving him the victory. [109]

Let us all unite more earnestly in imploring God's aid in fighting our battles for us. The thought that there are so many of God's people praying for His blessing upon the army greatly strengthens and encourages me. The Lord has answered their prayers, and my trust is in Him, that He will continue to do so. If God be for us, who can be against us? That He will still be with us and give us victory until our independence shall be established, and that He will make our nation that people who God is the

Lord, is my earnest and oft-repeated prayer. While we attach so much importance to being free from temporal bondage, we must attach far more to being free from the bondage of sin." [110]

In his assurance in battle, in his counseling others when they were troubled, one hears him resonate the psalmists strain,

He only is my rock and my salvation: he is my defense I shall not be moved. In God is my salvation and glory: the rock of my strength, and my refuge, is in God. Trust in him at all times: ye people, pour out your heart before him: God is a refuge for us. Psalm 62:6-8 [111]

When others, such as his wife, experienced difficulties in the face of opposition, he urged them to continue to trust and hope; he encouraged them.

"You must not be discouraged at the slowness of recovery. Look up to Him who giveth liberally for faith to be resigned to His divine will. And trust Him for that measure of health which will most glorify Him and advance to the greatest extent your own real happiness. We are sometimes suffered to be in a state of perplexity, that our faith may be tried and grow stronger. All things work together for good to God's children." [112]

"Try to look up and be cheerful, and not desponding. Trust our kind Heavenly father, and by the eye of faith see that all things with you are right and for your best interest. The clouds come, pass over us, and are followed by bright sunshine; so, in God's moral dealings with us, He permits us to have trouble awhile. But let us, even in the most trying dispensations of His providence, be cheered by the brightness which is a little ahead. Try to live near to Jesus, and secure that peace which flows like a river." [113]

Trust in the Lord for ever: for in the Lord Jehovah is everlasting strength. Isaiah 26:4 [114]

Those who knew him felt that he truly believed that God was responsible for all the consequences of his actions. He prayed to God for advice. God heard and answered, and guided him. He did as God lead him to and so God was deserving of all the praise and glory. Mrs. Graham of Winchester wrote Mrs. Jackson...

'Them that honor me, I will honor', is His own promise, and He has been faithful to his word. I think our dear general more entirely forgets self in his desire to glorify God than anyone I ever knew – his humble confiding trust in the Almighty gives me more comfort and more confidence than anything else. [115]

Jackson wrote this formal order to his troops,

"But his chief duty, and that of the army, is to recognize devoutly the hand of a protecting Providence in the brilliant successes of the last three days – which have given us the results of a great victory without great losses – and to make the oblation of our thanks to God for his mercies to us and our country in heartfelt acts of religious worship." [116]

When a leader relies on God they are confident. This confidence leads to greater focus and boldness. As seen in studying the lives of Lee and Jackson this leads to victory. Victories in turn increase followers' belief in the leader. They grow in their trust in him. This unifies, and adds to their own confidence. This in turn strengthens their efforts, and increases the organization's potential for success and victory.

Jackson justly gave God the credit in his official military reports, as is seen in this his last one:

"For these great and signal victories our sincere and humble thanks are due unto Almighty God. We should in all things acknowledge that hand of him who reigns in heaven and rules among the armies of men...We can but express the grateful conviction of our mind that God was with us and gave us the victory, and unto His holy name be the praise." [117]

Trust in the Lord with all thine heart; and lean not unto thine own understanding. In all thy ways acknowledge him, and he shall direct thy paths. [118]

Jackson writes in a letter to his wife,

"I am again retiring before the enemy. They endeavored to get in my rear by moving on both flanks of my gallant army, but our God has been my guide and saved me from their grasp." [119]

There are real and glorious blessings, I trust, in reserve for us beyond this life. It is best for us to keep our eyes fixed upon the throne of God and the realities of a far more glorious existence beyond the verge of time. It is gratifying to be beloved and to have our conduct approved by our fellow-men, but this is not worthy to be compared with the glory that is in reservation for us in the presence of our glorified Redeemer. Let us endeavor to adorn the doctrine of Christ our Savior in all things, knowing that there awaits us a far more exceeding and eternal weight of glory. I would not relinquish the slightest diminution of that glory for all this world can give. My prayer is that such may ever be the feeling of my heart. [120]

If one trusts that God is the wisest and best counselor, and if one wishes to do the best one can then, the greater the test, the greater the prayer. His servant, Jim said,

"The general is a great one for praying at all times. But when I see him get up a great many times in the night to pray, then I know there is going to be something to pay." [121]

If when we are severely tested and faced with immediate and pressing challenges, when crucial decisions demand wise action, if we then turn and return to the one who is never wrong, the wisest of counselors, one who knows all and cares about us, then how can we be troubled? Will we not in the midst of pressure and strife find the quietness and confidence trusting in God brings? In resting in Him we are able to make the best decisions, and all is saved.

Behold, God is my salvation; I will trust, and not be afraid: for the Lord Jehovah is my strength and my song; he also is my salvation Isaiah 12:2 [122]

For thus saith the Lord God, The Holy One of Israel; In returning and rest shall ye be saved; in quietness and confidence shall be your strength… *Isaiah 30:15* [123]

They that trust in the Lord shall be as mount Zion, which cannot be moved, but abideth forever. Psalm 125:1 [124]

CHAPTER VI.
A LEADER IS REVERENT

Thomas, "Stonewall", Jackson revered God. Remember our three pillars: God, Family, Vocation. One of these chief pillars is our relationship with God. The more you read of his life the more you come to see that his relationship with his God was much of what made Jackson, Jackson. We began at this reliance, and at his giving the credit to God, in the last chapter.

Harvey Hill an extraordinary believer himself, stated of Jackson, "The striking characteristic of his mind [became] his profound reverence for divine…authority. I never knew anyone whose reverence for Deity was so all pervading, and who felt so completely his entire dependence upon God." [125]

The dictionary defines reverence as deep respect, awe, even fear.

"Let all the earth fear (revere) the Lord; let all of the inhabitants of the world stand in awe of him." Psalm 33:8 [126]

"Behold, the eye of the Lord is upon them that fear (revere) him, upon them that hope in his mercy; to deliver their soul from death, and to keep them alive in famine. Psalm 33:18-19 [127]

"The fear of the Lord is the beginning of knowledge" Proverbs 1:7 [128]

The fear of the Lord is the beginning of wisdom." Proverbs 9:10 [129]

By humility and fear of the lord are riches, and honor, and life."
Proverbs 22:4 [130]

" Therefore thou shalt keep the commandments of the Lord thy God, to
walk in his ways, and to fear (revere) him." Deuteronomy 8:6 [131]

It says in Hebrews that God heard Abraham because he feared, revered God. So God listens to those who fear, respect, revere Him.

And from King Solomon the wisest and most successful of all men...

The fear of the Lord is the beginning of knowledge; Proverbs 1:7 [132]

Fear of the Lord leads to wisdom, and so we can seek His help in making the best decisions through prayer, and He will hear us, and answer.

We have come to see how the Bible was one of the books Jackson studied. It is likely he had read these verses and meditated upon their meaning for him, for all God's children. It is likely he would decide to conform himself, mold himself, into one who would be reverent to God. Yet even more, I cannot help but believe that, like Jackson, when one has honestly sought, and truly found God, one cannot help but be awed by him, by His power, wisdom, and righteousness; by His holiness, His being God. We are awed by His Holiness and our sinfulness; and by His forgiveness and paying the price of our sins for us.

Jackson revered God and sought His will.

"His whole nature and convictions were penetrated by a reverence for all constituted authority, and for right order in church and state." [133]

One of his minister friends compares his obedience to the minister's placing a task on him, to his seeing the minister as a superior officer, and so deserving of his obedience and respect. I remember a story about Peter Marshall, a former chaplain to the United States Congress, and how his wife said he referred to God as, "the Chief or the Boss." How likely it would have been for Jackson, the military man, to have seen God as his supreme commander.

I can imagine Jackson respecting God for His authority, and because reverence was wise and right. I feel having studied him that Jackson did honestly, earnestly, seek God until he found Him. And finding Him, with an open, sincere heart, he could not help but to be awed, and to come to deeply respect and revere this Almighty ruler of the universe.

But I sincerely believe that to Thomas Jackson God was more, GOD. Like no other. His God, his Father; one who cared for him more than any other ever would, that one who would never leave him, and that one who would some day bring him home to be with Him and his loved ones forevermore. HIS God whom he sought, found, knew and loved.

...the verse that most inspired him was Romans 8:28 "And we know that all things work together for good to them that love God, to them that are called according to his purpose." [134]

In one of Thomas Jackson's books we find,

"God constituted you for happiness, and that happiness is to be achieved only by deliberately choosing the service of the Lord as the great end of living." Joel Parker. Invitations to True Happiness, and Motives for Becoming a Christian. (New York, 1844) 10,34 [135]

He spoke emphatically of the duty of conforming our wills to God's, and of a thoroughly cheerful acquiescence whenever His will was manifested... His favorite maxim was: "Duty is ours; the consequences are God's." He spoke much also of the blessedness of a full and hearty obedience, in its effects upon the Christian's own happiness. [136]

It is easy to imagine that for Jackson, true happiness could only be found in seeking and doing God's will in all things. Thus reading the Bible to learn His will and praying to ask His will would be essential to true happiness and success in this life. In revering God, seeking and then adhering to His will.

He felt it his duty to adopt a strict code of moral conduct in order to live his religion every waking hour of the day. A starting point was systematic reading of the Bible and religious books. [137]

"We should always seek by prayer to be taught our duty." [138]

A cadet who came to know Jackson well concluded, "He laid every plan, purpose, and desire before his Great Master, implored his direction, and when assured what the will of God was, he never deviated one hair's breadth from the path of duty." [139]

Commensurate with church membership, he adopted the ancient Hebrew practice of tithing. He contributed 10 percent of his income to the church every remaining year of his life. [140]

He reserved Sunday as a day devoted only to the things of God. As his wife revealed she was to avoid any reference to secular topics on the Sabbath. If one arose, he would smile and say, "We will talk about that tomorrow." [141]

He would not write or have letters in transit on the Sabbath. [142]

He did not like to fight battles on the Sabbath,

"You appear greatly concerned about my attacking on Sunday. I was greatly concerned too; but I felt it my duty to do it, in consideration of the ruinous effects that might result from postponing the battle until the next morning.. So far as I can see my course was a wise one; the best that I could do under the circumstances, though very distasteful to my feelings, and I hope and pray to our heavenly father, that I may never again be circumstanced as on that day." [143]

In obedience to the old testament Jackson sought to keep the Sabbath holy by doing no work. And yet, influenced by new testament he too felt that like Jesus said in John 5:17, "my father goes on working and so do I." There were times that God's work had to be accomplished on the Sabbath.

Even in battle he sought God's will.

At a climatic moment Jackson came riding down the road, "His head was bowed and his right hand, gauntleted, was pointing upward. He was alone and seemed oblivious to all around him and presented the appearance of being in supplication and rendering thanks." [144]

Colonel Bradley T. Johnson of the First Maryland in an engagement realized the general was praying, "Abstracted, dead to the strife, and blind to all around, his soul communed alone with his God." [145]

"You that have seen Jackson fight ought to have heard Jackson pray. He did not pray to men but to God...He seemed to realize he was talking to Heaven's King." [146]

Recognizing the sovereignty of the Lord of Hosts, he interceded for his veterans, that "the Almighty would cover them with his feathers, and that his truth might be their shield and buckler." [147]

Reading of another Christian soldier one cannot help after studying Jackson to feel these comments are an echo to him as well. Of Captain Lewis Coleman it was said,

"Oh! If such concern were generally exhibited by officers, nominally pious, for the higher, the spiritual welfare of their men, how much more easily would they be controlled; how effectively restrained from wrong and encouraged in right. Do such exhibitions of solicitous piety weaken discipline? Rather do they strengthen it, by superadding a sense of obligation to the army regulations. Do they diminish courage? He is the bravest fighter, other things being equal, who has the firmest trust in God." [148]

To most of the men who were his troops Stonewall Jackson was... "greatest and noblest in that he was good, and...gave his talent and his life to a cause that, as before the God he so devotedly served, he deemed right and just." [149]

Thomas Jackson revered God. It was a large part of what made him the successful leader he was. Not only did it make him a more wise and conscientious leader, it made him a greater influence on his men.

This reverence, this fear of the Lord, this realizing his dependence on God also encouraged another trait of a great leader. The characteristic of humility and viewing all of what one does as service, a duty to serve God and others. This is perhaps best said in what I believe to be the greatest definition of true leadership.

"Ye know that the princes of the gentiles exercise dominion over them, and they that are great exercise authority upon them. But it shall not be so among you: whosoever will be great among you, let him be your minister; And whosoever will be chief among you, let him be your servant: Even as the son of man came not to be ministered unto, but to minister, and to give his life a ransom for many." Matthew 20:25-28 [150]

To be a leader, is to serve as Christ did. To so love others as to be willing to lay down your life for them. When one is a leader such as that, such as Lee and Jackson; Patton and Bradley and others were; to love ones people as one's children; then your people will achieve the impossible for you, at any cost. They will fight for this parent who cares for them, this good, just, wise, and reverent parent.

CHAPTER VII.

A LEADER IS HUMBLE, GIVES THE CREDIT AND PRAISE TO OTHERS; AND IS AT HEART A SERVANT.

Several things probably motivate leaders to be successful. We all want to win, to be successful in what we do. It is nice to be recognized as one of the best in our field. We all enjoy it when others place their trust in us and are willing to follow our lead. These result in our feeling better about ourselves. It can be argued that feeling good about ourselves is a strong motivator. And we might achieve even greater positive feeling through the greater gains achieved via leadership. The majority of us feel good when we help, or serve others. One could argue, however, that some may feel good when they oppress others, or cause others to serve them.

I believe we feel best when we serve others. When enrolled in college studying many different cultures and religions I was amazed to discover that all of the religions have one tenet or principle in common. "Do unto others what you would have them do unto you." Or perhaps one could rephrase it to "Serve others as you would have them serve you." I must confess it is hard to imagine anyone desiring to oppress or hurt others as you want to be oppressed or hurt. I believe that in truly great leaders, the basic motivation is to serve others. Yes, there have been infamous leaders, but it is generally the famous we are impressed by and want to be like. The good servant-leaders seem to achieve the more enduring changes, the greatest followings, the greater honor.

It is his or her dedication to those he or she serves, that causes the leader to desire the best information and advice, to make the best decision possible, to obtain the greatest benefits for those served. When you have a leader who goes before you into danger, who strives to obtain the best supplies and rations for you, who shares the trials with you; a leader who seeks to fight the best way possible in order to gain the most, with the least number being injured or killed; those led see that. They soon understand that the leader really cares about them.

The leader who weighs every decision based on its impact on his or her people, that one who seeks to gain the greatest benefits for all, who strives to avoid having to lay off as many as possible when things get tight, and who even goes the extra mile of trying to locate replacement positions for them, and providing some finances to help tide them over until they assume a new job, that one, will always be respected and followed. Even when these less than desirable things occur people will not forget the leaders caring. They will always be quick to spread the trustworthiness, and add to the renown and reputation for that leader.

It is this service, this love of others, that results in the respect, and love of their followers for them. It is this that causes their followers to go far beyond what is expected, to achieve far more than was thought possible.

Robert E. Lee was beyond a doubt a servant-leader. Omar Bradley certainly was and was called, "The soldier's soldier." Even George Patton, I believe, achieved all he did by caring for his soldiers. It was said they always had good clothing, shoes, rations, etc. To get really good results require a leader who cares about their people. Even though they were defeated. Even when their cause was lost, Lee's men still loved him. Even his opponents in the north revered him as a great leader.

Thomas Jackson was such a leader as well. Let's look at what we might learn from him, and his favorite book, about humility and being a servant leader.

"There was sometimes a softness and a tenderness about him that was very striking. Under every and all circumstances he never forgot that he was a Christian and acted up to his Christian faith unswervingly." [151]

Looking at various translations of the Bible, some define humble as afflicted...

"And the afflicted (humble) Thou (God) will save." II Samuel 22:28 [152]

"For thou wilt save the afflicted (humble) ; but will bring down high looks (haughtiness)." Psalm 18:27 [153]

Wherefore he sayeth, God resisteth the proud, but giveth grace unto the humble." James 4:6 [154]

So the implication is that pride, or haughtiness, leads to failure. It can be a real turn off to others. And pride may lead to over confidence and taking one too many, or one too great of a risk. Humility on the other hand impresses both God and others. A humble person is easy to listen to, and easy to like, and to trust.

Some translations equate humility with meekness ...

"The meek [humble] will he guide in judgment; and the meek [humble] he will teach his way." Psalm 25:9 [155]

The one who believes there is room to improve, will listen and grow. The one who thinks he knows it all, stops learning and soon fails.
"The Lord lifteth up the meek [humble]; he casteth the wicked down to the ground." Psalm 147:6 [156]

"For all those things hast mine hand made, and all those things have been, saith the Lord: but to this man will I look, even to him that is poor and of a contrite spirit, and trembleth at my word." Isaiah 66:2 [157]

Again we see that pride seems to be associated with wickedness. Indeed when someone boasts, don't they leave us feeling that they love themselves more than anyone else? It appears they think first of serving themselves, not others, and not us. I know I soon begin to develop feelings of distrust when I am forced to listen to someone tell me at great length how good they are, and what they have done. If they have to sell me, maybe it's not true. Doesn't it seem as though those who would earn our trust, gain it best by demonstrating, through service and consideration, that they deserve it?

"When pride cometh, then cometh shame: but with the lowly is wisdom."
Proverbs 11: 2 [158]

"The fear of the Lord is the instruction of wisdom; and before honor is humility." Proverbs 15:33 [159]

"Before destruction the heart of man is haughty, and before honor is humility." Proverbs 18:12 [160]

By humility and fear of the lord are riches, and honor, and life."
Proverbs 22:4 [161]

Pride, haughtiness, and boastfulness lead to destruction and shame. Humility, modesty, and reverence of God, lead to wisdom, honor and success. Developing humility and a servant nature as a leader will lead to our being successful. Let's look at Jackson. He was successful. Many countries' experts feel he was one of the greatest military leaders ever. We saw in the last chapter that he was reverent. Was he seen to be modest and humble by those who knew him?

"Modesty was among his greatest attractions." [162]

"Praise made Jackson genuinely uncomfortable." [163]

"His zeal and activity in the cause of religion were among his most striking characteristics." A cadet at the time noted. "Yet while he labored constantly he did so quietly and modestly." [164]

"Jackson resented praise, glory for his achievements belonged to God." [165]

"Jackson did not feel self-esteem... "after all, he was only the instrument of his Heavenly Father." [166]

"...he, with his characteristic modesty, gave all the credit to his noble men." [167]

"Thus always, whatever his army achieved, his modesty leads him to ascribe it to his brave men, feeling himself to be but a humble instrument in the hand of God." [168]

Jackson, as he left his brigade, gave them the praise and credit.

"In the Army of the Shenandoah you were the First Brigade; in the Army of the Potomac you were the First Brigade; in the Second Corps of this army you are the First brigade; you are the First brigade in the affections of your general; and I hope by your future deeds and bearing you will be handed down as the First Brigade in our second war of independence. Farewell!" [169]

Jackson told many people that the name, "Stonewall", and the associated fame belonged not to him but to his men.

Mrs. Graham of Winchester wrote Mrs. Jackson...

"Them that honor me, I will honor," is His own promise, and He has been faithful to His word. I think our dear general more entirely forgets self in his desire to glorify God than anyone I ever knew – his humble confiding trust in the Almighty gives me more comfort and more confidence than anything else. [170]

His family, noticed it, his neighbors, students, his men. All noticed it, and one senses, all gained from it. All gained a greater trust in him, a greater ability to work with him, to dare more, and strive more. Because of his humility, his giving others the credit rather than hoarding it for himself, he motivated others to excel. His reliance on God gave his people greater confidence. For these reasons those who knew him were able to accomplish more.

"for there was never a man with whom it was easier to keep on friendly terms than with him. He was not demonstrative, but he was one of the most obliging of men, ever willing to do any favor that might be asked of him, without any regard for his personal convenience." [171]

His modesty and humility did lead to others enjoying being with him. It made him easy to get along with, to cooperate with, to work with creating a synergy that lead to greater accomplishments than either could achieve alone.

How did he further manifest humility? How did he, by being a servant, gain even more trust and support?

His wife stated, "His heart was as soft as a woman's; he was full of love and gentleness." [172]

He was sensitive to others. He put himself on an equal plane with others. He never implied by word or act that he was more important or mattered more than others. On the contrary, in word and action he placed himself on the same plane as others.

"When it was suggested he take a furlough he replied, "I can't be absent, as my attention is necessary in preparing my troops for hard fighting, should it be required; and as my officers and soldiers are not permitted to visit their wives and families, I ought not to see mine." [173]

He further more did not only demonstrate that he was their equal, not superior, but showed that he cared about them. He cared enough to be aware of their needs, and to put these before his own.

Once he fed General Jeb Stuart and his Major Von Borcke and then put them up in his tent. In the morning they awoke to a figure placing a basin of water and a towel at Von Borcke's head.

"Now major," the man said, "wash quickly. A cup of coffee is waiting for you, your horse is saddled, and you must be off at once." The Prussian then realized that his "servant" was Jackson. The light touch had been given by the iron hand, and the soft voice was that which had been heard...amid the tumult of battle. I shall never forget the smile that broke over his kindly face at my amazement in recognizing him." [174]

Once when his friend Colonel Boteler was sleeping in his tent, he observed…

"…after sleeping profoundly for two or three hours, he [Jackson] rose, lighted his candle, and continued his writing [dispatches]. In glancing around he noted that the light of his candle shone full upon the face of his friend, whom he supposed to be still sleeping, and with the quick thoughtfulness of a woman he placed a book upon his table in front of the candle, so as to shield his face from the light and not interrupt his slumber." [175]

A certain captain in the English army came to see him being completely

drenched from the weather and noted this incident…

The general, who is indescribably simple and unaffected in all his ways, took up my wet overcoat with his own hands, made up the fire, brought wood for me to put my feet on to keep them warm while my boots were drying, and began to ask me questions on various subjects. At the dinner-hour we went out and joined the members of his staff. At this meal the general said grace in a fervent, quiet manner, which struck me very much…In the morning, at breakfast-time I noticed that the general said grace before the meal with the same fervor I had remarked before…He said, 'Captain I have been trying to dry your great-coat, but I am afraid I have not succeeded very well.' That little act illustrates the man's character. With the care and responsibility of a vast army on his shoulders, he finds time to do little acts of kindness and thoughtfulness, which make him the darling of his men, who never seem to tire talking of him." [176]

Once a mother asked him to bless her young child.

"If the request seemed out of order to some members of the staff, it was not so with Jackson. While still seated on Little Sorrel, "the warrior-saint of another era, with the child in his arms, head bowed until his graying beard touched the fresh young hair of the child, pressed close to the shabby coat that had so well been acquainted with death…closed his eyes, and seemed to be…occupied for a minute or two with prayer, during

which we took off our hats and the young mother leaned her head over the horse's shoulder as if uniting in the prayer. Jackson finished and gently returned the baby to the mother. She thanked him with streaming eyes while he rode off back down the road." [177]

While staying at the Corbin residence he became a friend to one of their daughters, Janie.

"Her love for the general matched his affection for her. Staff members were amazed at the sight of the two. One moment their stern, humorless leader was saying of the Federals: 'We must do more than defeat their armies; we must destroy them.' The next moment he was a tender companion frolicking with a small child. Many people came to the Moss Neck headquarters with the thought that Jackson was incapable of open displays of love. Then they witnessed his uninhibited behavior with a little girl who adored every minute of it, and the visitors went away either perplexed or with a more positive opinion of the field commander." [178]

The reverend Dabney relates this incident while at Reverend D.B. Ewing's house involving one of Rev. Ewing's children,

"One of these, while sitting upon his knee, was captivated with the bright military buttons upon his coat, and petitioned that when the garment was worn out, he should give her one as a keepsake. This he promised; and month afterward, amidst all his weighty cares, he remembered to send her the gift;" [179]

His wife relates the following story to demonstrate his kindness and the tenderness of his heart…

A gentleman who spent the night with us was accompanied by his daughter, but four years of age. It was the first time the child had been separated from her mother, and my husband, fearing she might miss the watchfulness of a woman's heart, suggested that she should be committed

to my care during the night, but she clung to her father. After his guests had both sunk into slumber, the father was aroused by someone leaning over his little girl and drawing the covering more closely around her. It was only his thoughtful host, who felt anxious lest his little guest should miss her mother's guardian care under his roof, and he could not go to sleep himself until he was satisfied that all was well with the child." [180]

Dr. Hunter McGuire relates an incident.

"As Jackson rode along with his staff he was accosted by a poor, plain country woman to know if he was "Mr. Jackson." And if the troops in the road were his "company." The army then probably consisted of thirty thousand men. It was of course made up of divisions, brigades, and regiments, and a great many companies, but this woman only knew that her son "John" belonged to Jackson's company," and she expressed a great deal of surprise when General Jackson told her that he didn't know the boy. "What," she said, "don't you know John_____? He has been with you a year, and I brought him these socks and something to eat." She began to cry bitterly. Some members of the staff were disposed to laugh, but Jackson stopped them, got down from his horse and tried to explain to the woman how it was impossible that he should know her son, a simple private in the ranks, but she persisted he must know him, and she must see him, and that she had spent a great deal of time in fixing these things for him. He asked her what county the boy came from. He sent for Colonel Alexander swift ["Sandie"] Pendleton and asked him what companies were in his army from that county. He then sent three or four couriers to each one of the companies from that county, and found the boy and brought him to the woman, who gave him the presents she had for him." [181]

Perhaps of greatest importance these acts of love and caring, this serving of others, placing them before self, was not wasted on his men who grew to love him and risk all for him. His international enduring fame and reputation is a result of all they accomplished, catalyzed by his love for, and serving of, them.

"How anxious he was for his army! I could not detect the slightest trace of self-importance, ostentation, or seeking after vain glory. To glorify God possessed all his thoughts." [182]

Jackson did not just care for the men's physical needs, he also cared about their spiritual welfare as beautifully related in the book, "Christ in the Camp." Jackson would spend his Sunday's encouraging church services. He promoted the handing out of religious tracts and was instrumental in the formation of The Chaplain's Association. Jackson strove to obtain the best ministers possible for his army. He was most anxious that his men be not only soldiers for his country, but also soldiers of the cross. In all things his care for his men resembles the care of a father for his children.

Three persons related the story of Jackson once standing guard over his exhausted men while they slept.

Colonel John Preston relates…

"At the battle of First Manassas the victory was decided in our favor by the cooperation of the armies of Johnson and Beauregard. Johnson's army leaving their camps, leaving their foe in front of them suddenly crossed the mountains and by his forced marches first gained for Jackson's troops the name of foot cavalry. Jackson, that night, ordered out his usual pickets, but the officer of the guard told him that the soldiers were all asleep completely exhausted—and asked whether he should arouse them. 'No.' replied the general, 'let our men sleep. I will watch the camp,' and

silently he rode around that sleeping host, the only sentinel until the day broke in the east." [183]

John Newton Lyle writes…

"It was at this halt that General Jackson told the officer of the day not to mount the guard, but to let the men rest, and that he would watch while the brigade slept…he was too considerate of others to make a lazy aide get out and do something unusual." [184]

Jackson's wife relates from his letters to her,

…About two o'clock in the morning we arrived at the little village of Paris, where we remained sleeping until nearly dawn. I mean the troops slept, as my men were so exhausted that I let them sleep while I kept watch myself." [185]

And again she shares,

"After pacing around the camp, or leaning upon the fence, watching the slumbers of his men until nearly daylight, he yielded his post to a member of his staff, who insisted on relieving him, and he then threw his wearied frame down upon a bed of leaves in a fence corner and snatched an hour or two of sleep." [186]

Captain Hugh White said,

" I have learned to look up to him with implicit confidence, and to approach him with perfect freedom, being always assured of a kind and attentive hearing." [187]

"If he passed a spot where some of his men lay dead, their blood still wet and red, he would draw in the little sorrel and raise his hand as if he were a priestly crusader who prayed for the souls of the fallen and blessed them for their valor. [188]

"A time comes in all protracted operations when the nervous energy of the best troops becomes exhausted, when the most daring shrink from further sacrifice, when the desire of self-preservation infects the stoutest veterans, and the will of the mass imposes a tacit resistance to all further effort. "Then," says Clauswitz, "the spark in the breast of the commander must rekindle hope in the hearts of his men, and so long as he is equal to this he remains their master. When his influence ceases and his own spirit is no longer enough to revive the spirit of others, the masses, drawing him with them, sink into that lower region of animal nature which recoils from danger and knows not shame. Such are the obstacles which the brain and the courage of the military commander must overcome if he is to make his name illustrious." [189]

Isn't it amazing? Humility, and the placing of oneself, not above others, but equal to, even below them, as their servant, results in them trusting you, following you, and risking far more, striving far more, than they ever would have without you as their servant-leader.

"Whoever wishes to be great among you must be your servant." Amplified *Matthew 20:26* [190]

Want to be great? To make a difference. To be a leader long remembered in a positive way? Serve those around you at home, work and in your community, and those you meet in this life. Then perhaps, some day, someone will use you to demonstrate how to be a leader.

CHAPTER VIII.

A LEADER ADMITS HIS SHORTCOMINGS AND STRIVES TO OVERCOME THEM.

We have talked about a leader not being wise in his own eyes and trusting in those wiser. We have looked at humility and giving the credit to our team and God. Now we will look at something very closely related to these, admitting our shortcomings and striving to change, to grow, to correct our mistakes.

These concepts are very closely related. It is a sign of growth and maturity to realize that we can't do it alone. No one knows it all. No one can see the entire big picture. With a team of others to provide the best data possible, and by seeking the advice of a multitude of good counselors, we obtain a clearer picture, and a greater appreciation of all possibilities. The final decision and action may be ours, but the data and advice increases our ability to make a good decision.

When we give others the credit due them we demonstrate that they have worth and increase their confidence and performance. We show them that we see and appreciate what they do. We show them we are trustworthy in that we don't take all the credit for ourselves, but in fact give credit where it is due. This increases their faith in us. It strengthens our relationship and allows us to work better together, to achieve together more than we could achieve working separately.

When we acknowledge our shortcomings we admit to ourselves and others that we are not perfect; and that we need others. When we admit this to ourselves, we are able to be humble. We are aware of our weaknesses and are better able to take them into consideration. We are less likely to make mistakes. We are also more apt to truly listen to others, and to value their views and insights, and so better weigh and act on them. We are less likely to act rashly and more likely to make better, wiser decisions.

When we admit to ourselves and others that we need them, again, we build their self-image, self-esteem and confidence. They are grateful for this. They risk more and achieve more. The result is a stronger relationship, a stronger bond.

No one achieves much by themselves. It can be argued that the more people we work with, the greater the size of our team, the greater difference we can make. The greater number of people we influence, the greater impact of our team on our society. However, the bigger the team, then the more people we have to admit our shortcomings to, and confess our mistakes to.

If we can find the courage and honesty to admit our own mistakes, then we impact a greater number of people. We gain the trust of more people, we increase the self-respect, and self-worth of more people. We strengthen and bind together a greater team. This team's greater cohesion then, and loyalty, and strength, is more likely to have a far more effective and greater impact. Isn't that great! The harder the task, the greater the self-sacrifice, the greater the impact and results.

When Solomon became King of Israel the first thing he did was pray and ask God for greater wisdom to rule his people. He asked it for his people's sake. In return for his admitting his inadequacy and need for help to himself and God, (and others in accepting the advice of his father David and counselors), he became the wisest, wealthiest, most successful leader recorded in the Bible.

So though the task may be hard, that of admitting we were wrong or made a mistake, the rewards are increased effectiveness and success. Let's see what Solomon and other successful leaders have to say about it.

Solomon and his father, David, touched on this subject from several angles and tell us:

"Be not wise in thine own eyes: fear the Lord, and depart from evil."
Proverbs 3:7 [191]

"My son, despise not the chastening of the Lord: neither be weary of his correction; For whom the lord loveth he correcteth; even as a father the son in whom he delighteth." Psalm 3:11-12 [192]

"For the commandment is a lamp; and the law is a light; and reproofs of instruction are the way of life:" Psalm 6:23 [193]

"The way of a fool is right in his own eyes; but he that hearkeneth unto counsel is wise." Proverbs 12:15 [194]

"Only by pride cometh contention; but with the well advised is wisdom." Proverbs 13:10 [195]

"Every prudent man deals with knowledge, but a self-confident fool exposes and flaunts his folly." Proverbs 13:10 [196]

"Every prudent man dealeth with knowledge: but a fool layeth open his folly." Proverbs 13:16 [197]

"Poverty and shame shall be to him that refuseth instruction: but he that regardeth reproof shall be honored." Proverbs 13:18 [198]

"The ear that heareth the reproof of life abideth among the wise. He that refuseth instruction despiseth his own soul: but he that heareth reproof getteth understanding." Psalm 15:31-32 [199]

"Hear counsel, and receive instruction, that thou mayest be wise in the latter end." Proverbs 19:20 [200]

"He that covereth his sins shall not prosper: but whoso confesseth and forsaketh them shall have mercy." Proverbs 28:13 [201]

Was Jackson a man who could admit and address his shortcomings? When he failed miserably at his attempts at public speaking he acknowledged this and persevered until he improved. Likewise when he failed in praying in public his minister attempted to spare him from embarrassment by not calling on him. He went to his minister and learning this was so he expressed the belief it was his duty and he must not shirk it. He said,

"If it is my duty to lead in prayer, then I must persevere in it until I learn to do it aright." [202]

He actually asked to be called on more, even though it was initially painfully embarrassing. And so he developed this ability and eventually became highly accomplished and greatly appreciated by his fellow church members.

Being able to laugh at oneself is the epitome of accepting ones shortcomings.

"Jackson marched his class to the parade ground one afternoon, announced that the institute's clock was incorrect, and that he would show them how to determine the time by observation with his instruments. It was shortly past noon at the time, but Jackson, after a series of calculations, announced the hour as seven PM, and cadets fell all about him, howling in laughter at the error made ludicrous by the man of legend Jackson had become. The Major joined in the laughter." [203]

One final note. If we look closely at all their stories, David's, Solomon's,

Stonewall Jackson's, we see that they all made mistakes. They all had shortcomings. David commits adultery and murder and creates trouble by not being the father he should have been. Solomon seeks more and more wives and is lead astray by them to worship other gods, to be unfaithful to His God and lead his country astray. Jackson fails to communicate as well as possible, and perhaps to be a bit more tolerant and accepting of others at times creating some strife in his army. He pushes himself too hard and as a consequence suffers from fatigue that results in poorer performance during the battles to defend Richmond. None of us are perfect. We all make mistakes. That should make it a bit easier to admit our shortcomings, to acknowledge mistakes, to correct them as we can. Now, if we can accept the forgiveness of others, and ourselves, then we can continue to go forward, be victorious, achieve, and make a difference for our world.

David admitted his mistakes, confessed them to God and his team, and the negative impact on his mission and his people was lessened. If we can admit our mistakes, confess them, and accept the consequences and forgiveness, we too can minimize the negative effect on our mission. And, with the help of God and our team, still achieve and be successful in our missions, like David and Thomas Jackson.

CHAPTER IX.

A LEADER SETS AND MAINTAINS HIS PRIORITIES

"Wisdom crieth without; she uttereth her voice in the streets: She crieth in the chief place of the concourse, in the openings of the gates: in the city she uttereth her words, saying, How long ye simple ones will ye love simplicity?" Proverbs 1:20-22 [204]

It is easy to miss wisdom. It is easy to get sidetracked in this life. In the introduction we talked about the importance of balance. We looked at three core pillars on which to build our lives. Relationship with God, relationship with family, vocation/relationship with others. We considered how essential it was to focus on these and later to maintain the proper priorities of God, Family, and Others if we wanted to succeed in life. Throughout this book we have looked at having these as our focus and then seeking to grow in all these areas, setting goals, making plans, and acting to achieve these goals. Yet we find that it is all to easy to get distracted.

The city street, the gates of commerce, the chief places of our work, these places are busy, and noisy. We are pushed by responsibilities and hustled and hassled by urgent demands. The voice of Wisdom and our priorities may be drowned out by the loudness of minute to minute challenges.

In focusing on the trees of problems and achievement, it is all too easy to lose sight of the forest of goals. In looking at the What, and How we can lose sight of the Why, and Who.

I for one have seen the men of our society taught that their chief role is to provide for their families. Men who then struggle so hard to do well at work and achieve to provide for their family that they have no time with their family, no time for God. The How and What, have blinded them to the Why and the Who.

I have seen men feel called by God to serve Him, family and country, yet become so focused on tasks that they soon see the tasks as the goal, the reason for all they do. Again they forget who they are striving for, why they sacrifice their time and strength and physical health, and even life.

One of the best quotes I have read, that helped me overcome this was... "I have never seen a man who on his death bed said, 'I wish I had spent more time at work." No they all would have spent more time with those they loved, and who loved them. Robertson shares this insight from one of Jackson's books,

"God constituted you for happiness, and that happiness is to be achieved only by deliberately choosing the service of the Lord as the great end

of living." Joel Parker. Invitations to True happiness, and Motives for Becoming a Christian. (New York, 1844), 10, 134. [205]

And again Robertson tells us,

*Jackson would have agreed with educator Charles W. Eliot's assertion that, " the security and elevation of the family and of family life are the prime objects of civilization, and the ultimate end of all industries." * [206]

How can we avoid losing sight of our priorities, of wandering off the path? One way is to read of others and learn from their successes and failures. Another is to set goals and priorities that we then constantly set before us and remind ourselves that this is our focus. Perhaps the best way is to use the same manual that Lee and Jackson and Patton and others have used to guide them through life and keep them on course, the Bible. A book of loving advice, a book filled with stories of others and how they failed and succeeded. A book that helps one see and set and remember priorities that lead to a successful life lived.

"The prudent man looketh well to his going." Proverbs 14:15 [207]

"I have taught thee in the way of wisdom; I have lead thee in right paths. When thou goest thy steps shall not be straightened; and when thou runnest, thou shalt not stumble." Proverbs 4:11-12 [208]

"Commit thy works to the Lord and thy thoughts shall be established." Proverbs 16:3 [209]

"A prudent man forseeth the evil and hideth himself: but the simple pass on, and are punished. Proverbs 22:3 [210]

Put First things First

"Prepare thy work without, and make it fit for thyself in the field; and afterwards build thine house. Proverbs 24:27 [211]

It is also important to realize that sometimes the fruits of success can lead us astray. We can get so wrapped up in enjoying the fruits of victory and in self-indulgence that we again forget our priorities.

"Let thine eyes look right on, and let thine eyelids look straight before thee. Ponder the path of thy feet, and let all thy way be established. Turn not to the right hand nor to the left: remove thy foot from evil."
Proverbs 4:26-27 [212]

"Folly is joy to him that is destitute of wisdom: but a man of understanding walketh uprightly." Proverbs 15:21 [213]

And what of Jackson? How was he at keeping focused and pursuing his priorities?

" 'Under the grave and generally serious nature,' Hunter McGuire stated, 'there was an intense earthly ambition....Ambition! Yes, far beyond what ordinary men possess. And yet, he told me when talking in my tent one dreary winter night....that he would not exchange one moment of his life hereafter, for all the earthly glory he could win'. " [214]

"...within the past years, I have endeavored to live more nearly unto God. And now nothing earthly could induce me to return to the world again... For my part, I am willing to go hence when it shall be his great will to terminate my earthly career. ...Rather than violate the known will of God, I would forfeit my life. It may seem strange to you, but nevertheless such a resolution I have taken, and I will by it abide." [215]

"My opinion is, that everyone should honestly and carefully investigate the Bible; and if he can believe it to be the word of God, to follow its teachings." [216]

"We should always seek by prayer to be taught our duty." [217]

"Never take counsel of your fears." [218]

He did not allow either success or fear of failure to lead him astray.

He avoided alcohol because he said, "I like it, and that's the reason I don't drink it." [219]

He did not surrender to selfish desires and tastes, but kept his focus. Leaders can grow to have a wide range of influence. Keep your focus and your people are more likely to keep their focus and stay on the right path as well. When you set your priorities and adhere to them; when you sacrifice self and personal gain to do what is right, your people follow your example and obtain success in their lives. When you become a leader such as this even your enemies praise you. In regards to Jackson, even the Northern press acknowledged his good character. After his death the newspaper, The Whig, wrote:

"What others did or attempted from impulses ambition, patriotism, or sense of duty, he did from compulsion of conscience, and a reverential conviction of obligation to his maker." [220]

Jackson still offers us this advice,

"Disregard public opinion when it interferes with your duty. Sacrifice your life rather than your word." [221]

A friend was once conversing with him about the difficulty of obeying the Scripture injunction, "Pray without ceasing," and Jackson insisted that we could so accustom ourselves to it that it could easily be obeyed. "When we take our meals there is the grace. When I take a draught of water I always pause, as my palate receives the refreshment, to lift up my heart to God in thanks and prayer for the water of life. Whenever I drop a letter into the box at the post-office I send a petition along with it for God's blessing upon its mission and upon the person to whom it is sent. When I break the seal of a letter just received I stop to pray to God that He may prepare me for its contents and make it a messenger of good. When I go to my classroom and await the arrangement of the cadets in their places, that is my time to intercede with God for them. And so of every other familiar act of the day." "But," said his friend, "do you not often forget these seasons coming so frequently?" "No!" said he. "I have made the practice habitual to me; and I can no more forget it than forget to drink when I am thirsty. The habit has become as delightful as regular." [222]

The Christian should carry his religion into everything. Christianity makes a man better in any lawful calling; it makes the general a better commander, and the shoemaker a better workman. In the case of a cobbler, or the tailor, for instance, religion will produce more care in promising work, more punctuality, and more fidelity in executing it, from conscientious motives; and these homely examples were fair illustrations of its value in more exalted functions. So, prayer aids any man, in any lawful business, not only by bringing down the divine blessing, which is its direct and primary object, but by harmonizing his own mind and heart. In the commander of an army at the critical hour, it calms his perplexities, moderates his anxieties, steadies the scales of judgment, and thus preserves him from exaggerated and rash conclusions. [223]

Keep your focus. Don't lose it despite trials and accolades and temptations. Focus on the "why" and the "who" you strive for.

"For what is a man profited, if he shall gain the whole world, and lose his own soul?" Matthew 16:26 [224]

The Bible is the greatest success text ever written. I like to refer to it as the,

"**B**ook of **I**nstruction for **B**uilding **L**eaders **E**veryday."

CHAPTER X.
A LEADER IS JUST AND IMPARTIAL

"Justice –Wrong none by doing injuries or omitting the benefits that are your duty." [225]

Justice, being just, the task of rewarding effort and achievement and correcting errors. Justice is hard work. It is caring enough to ever be observant. A leader must strive to notice their peoples' efforts, their striving to do their job. When your people give more than what is expected, go beyond the call, then you as their leader must show your appreciation for a job well done. To fail to notice and reward is to risk losing their going the extra mile and the momentum it can create for your organization. Being just, is also the less pleasant task of addressing errors, and discouraging mediocre efforts, and when needed, punishing the shirking of duty, failing to do what's needed and expected.

"To do justice is more disgraceful than to suffer it." – Plato [226]

The hardest price of leadership is the misunderstanding and misjudgment you may receive from being just and disciplining your people. Correction is painful and those corrected don't always accept their need for it and may become hurt and angry. Stonewall Jackson was strict, and at times felt by his people to be unduly strict. One of his men said something to the effect that in regards to desertion Jackson would have a man shot at the drop of a hat if he had to drop it himself. A minister at one time questioned his punishing a man in accordance with regulations feeling he should be merciful. Even when upholding what was right was unpopular Jackson did what had to be done to enforce regulations and see that his men performed their duty for their country.

Lt. Kyd Douglas in his book, "I Rode with Stonewall", wrote...

"General Jackson was as hard as nails; in the performance of duty he always was...[Although] a gentleman of tender influences and kind heart, he seemed to have a horror of cruelty. Why was this? Simply because in duty he was governed by his sense of justice, by the demands of public service. There was no place for sentiment or pity. In the execution of the law he was inexorable, justice and mercy seemed out of place." [227]

When you truly strive to consistently be fair, to seek the best for the organization and for everyone involved, eventually you will be admired and your efforts valued by your people. Reverend R. L. Dabny observed,

"To his Colonels he was a stricter master than to his private soldiers; and to his Generals, more exacting than to his Colonels. If he found in an officer a hearty and zealous purpose to do all his duty, with a willing and self-sacrificing courage and devotion, he was, to him, the most tolerant and gracious of superiors. But if he believed that his subordinates were self-indulgent or contumacious [rebellious], he became a stern and

exacting master, seeming ever to watch for an opportunity to visit their shortcomings upon them." [228]

Justice and discipline must be evenly meted out to build rather than destroy a sense of being a team. As one of his men said,

We do not look upon him merely as our commander – do not regard him as a severe disciplinarian, as a politician, as a man seeking popularity – but as a Christian; a brave man who appreciates the condition of a common soldier; as a fatherly protector; as one who endures all hardships in common with his followers; who never commands others to face danger without putting himself in the van. [229]

Because Jackson manifested humility and caring in all he did, his people saw his actions in their true light and respected him. As another said,

He never appointed a man to a responsible position without knowing all about him. He would make the most minute inquiries. Was he intelligent? Was he faithful? Was he industrious? Did he get up early? This was a great point with him. If a man was wanting in any of these qualifications, he would reject him, however highly recommended. No feeling of personal partiality, no feeling of friendship, was allowed to interfere with his duty. He felt that the interests at stake were too great to be sacrificed to favoritism or friendship. [230]

Jackson's people saw his character, his true motives and appreciated his justness and efforts.

"He had long cultivated the habit of connecting the most trivial and customery acts with silent prayer." [231]

If he demanded the strictest compliance with is instructions, he was always content to leave their execution to the judgment of his generals; and with supreme confidence in his own capacity, he was still sensible that

*his juniors in rank might be just as able. His supervision was constant,
but his interference rare; and it was not till some palpable mistake
had been committed that he assumed direct control of his divisions or
brigades.* [232]

Once your people are rewarded and disciplined and honed into competent team members you must then trust them with tasks and demonstrate your faith in them.

*His whole nature and convictions were penetrated by a reverence for all
constituted authority, and for right order in church and state.* [233]

To be just, to be fair and impartial, are traits of a successful leader. To die to self and act according to what is right and just alone. Why is this so important in a leader? When a leader manifests this trait of impartiality his or her followers know that they will be treated fairly. One will not be promoted over another because of favoritism. Their contributions are what determine their rewards and promotions. The leader's justice frees his subordinates to do their best with hope of recognition and reward.

*His wife said of him, "He was utterly free from censoriousness, envy,
detraction, and all uncharitableness, and certainly kept his rule that if he
could not say something good of a man, he would not speak of him at
all."* [234]

Justice and impartiality do not go necessarily hand in hand with the quality of mercy, but the results obtained by being merciful likewise benefit the mission of the organization. Justice frees the team member to do his or her best without fear that someone else will get the credit or rewards. Mercy frees the subordinate to take risks and make mistakes without being removed from the organization. If they error they might be forgiven and might be given another chance. So like justice, mercy is a trait in the leader that frees the subordinate to do their best. To be a successful leader one needs to sacrifice ones feelings and do what is right, acting impartially; and not holding a grudge or overreacting to mistakes made. Then the team can work to their best capacity to achieve the most possible for the leader. We feel more secure when our leaders act morally and justly; and when they demonstrate the quality of mercy.

We also respect them more when we see them apply the same rules to themselves. Not showing favoritism when they look into the mirror but treating that person the same as their subordinates are treated.

> *But if he carried his conscientiousness to extremes, if he laid down stringent rules for his own governance, he neither set himself up for a model nor did he attempt to force his convictions upon others. He was always tolerant; he knew his own faults, and his own temptations, and if he could say nothing good of a man he would not speak of him at all.* [235]

Solomon and others in the Bible demonstrate the quality of mercy, and often link it to caring for the less fortunate, and of caring for those in their control. Again the leader does not see himself as one who has power to use

people for helping to attain things, but one who as the power to use things

to help people.

A righteous man regardeth the life of his beast: but the tender mercies of the wicked are cruel." Proverbs 12:10 [236]

"The righteous considereth the cause of the poor," Proverbs 29:7 [237]

"The king that faithfully judgeth the poor, his throne shall be established forever." Proverbs 29:14 [238]

" Ye shall not afflict any widow or fatherless child." Exodus 22:22 [239]

"Learn to do well; seek judgment, relieve the oppressed, judge the fatherless, plead for the widow." Isaiah 1:17 [240]

"Thus saith the Lord; execute ye judgment and righteousness, and deliver the spoiled out of the hand of the oppressor: and do no wrong, do no violence to the stranger, the fatherless, nor the widow, neither shed innocent blood in this place." Jeremiah 21:3 [241]

What do David and Solomon have to say about the outcome for leaders

who are just and merciful…

"For the Lord loveth justice, and forsaketh not his saints; they are preserved forever: but the seed of the wicked shall be cut off." Psalm 37:28 [242]

"The curse of the Lord is in the house of the wicked; but he blesseth the habitation of the just." Proverbs 3:33 [243]

"The fear of the wicked, it shall come upon him; but the desire of the righteous shall be granted." Proverbs 10:24 [244]

"The righteous shall never be removed: but the wicked shall not inhabit the earth." Proverbs 10:30 [245]

Riches profit not in the day of wrath: but righteousness delivereth from death." Proverbs 11:4 [246]

The righteousness of the perfect shall direct his way: but the wicked shall fall by his own wickedness. Proverbs 11:5 [247]

"Evil pursueth sinners: but to the righteous good shall be repaid." Proverbs 13:21 [248]

"Better is a little with righteousness than great revenues without right." Proverbs 16:8 [249]

"To do justice and judgement is more acceptable to the lord than sacrifice." Proverbs 21:3 [250]

"It is joy to the just to do judgement: but destruction shall be to the workers of iniquity" Proverbs 21:15 [251]

"He that followeth after righteousness and mercy findeth life, righteousness and honor." Proverbs 21:21 [252]

"To show partiality is not good." Proverbs 28:21 [253]

"Blessed are they that keep judgment, and he that doeth righteousness at all times." Psalm 106:3 [254]

"For thou, Lord, wilt bless the righteous; with favor wilt thou compass him as with a shield." Psalms 5:12 [255]

"For the righteous Lord loveth righteousness; his countenance doth behold the upright." Psalm 11:7 [256]

I have been young, and now am old; yet have I not seen the righteous forsaken, nor his seed begging bread. Psalm 37:25 [257]

"The righteous shall be glad in the Lord, and shall trust in him; and all the upright in heart shall glory. Psalm 64:10 [258]

"In his days shall the righteous flourish; and abundance of peace so long as the moon endureth. Psalm 72:7 [259]

"Unto the upright there ariseth light in the darkness: he is gracious, and full of compassion and righteous." Psalm 112:4 [260]

Leaders who are just and merciful achieve success and are better able to overcome when challenges arise.

We have seen how the leader being just and merciful frees the team member to work harder to achieve more for the organization. Are there benefits to the team member who is disciplined by a just and impartial leader?

"For whom the Lord loveth he correcteth..." Proverbs 3:12 [261]

"...and reproofs of instruction are the way of life." 6:23 [262]

"He that spareth his rod hateth his son: but he that loveth him chasteneth him betimes [early]." Proverbs 13:24 [263]

The subordinate, or team member, who is corrected when they make a mistake profit from it in two ways.

First they are shown how to do the task properly enabling them to achieve more for themselves and the organization. Their time is not wasted, they are more profitable. Second, when you are disciplined for making a mistake, you also learn that what you do matters, that you matter. Children who are disciplined feel more secure and know their parents care about them. Subordinates are no different. They learn that it is better to be a team player, that what they do is noticed and that the leader cares about their performance, and about them.

It's obvious from what we've seen that Thomas Stonewall Jackson was a leader who was just and impartial, who noticed, who used discipline properly. Let's finish this chapter with some words from two other great leaders in history, and one quote from a less known leader . Listen to what they have to say about how to use discipline.

Robert E. Lee said,

"When a man makes a mistake, I call him to my tent, talk to him and use the authority of my position to make him do the right thing next time." [264]

"Discipline is based on pride in the profession of arms, on meticulous attention to details, on mutual respect and confidence. Discipline must be a habit so ingrained that it is stronger than the excitement of battle or the fear of death." General George S. Patton [265]

Discipline can only be obtained when all officers are so imbued with the sense of their awful obligation to their men and to their county that they cannot tolerate negligence. Officers who fail to correct errors or to praise excellence are valueless in peace and dangerous misfits in war." General George S. Patton [266]

"There is only one kind of discipline-perfect discipline. If you do not enforce and maintain discipline, you are potential murderers. You must set the example." General George S. Patton [267]

A quote of my own when teaching younger officers and non-commissioned officers about discipline was, "Discipline is like a wet stone used to hone a blade. It's purpose is to hone the members of the armed forces into a sharp sword for the defense of America. If it is not used when needed the sword becomes dull and rusty. If it is not used carefully, lovingly, it can blunt the blade, do more harm than good, even cause the sword to break, leaving America defenseless. To not learn how to use this wet stone, to neglect administering it properly is far more than unprofessional, it borders on treason, it robs America of her weapon of defense."

"Remember praise is more valuable than blame." General George S. Patton [268]

Praise is the best motivator. When you care enough to notice your people, to correct their errors and to praise their efforts, you invest yourself in them. You show them you care. The best way to see these things is to work with them. As you work with them, observe and talk with them about their efforts and reward their accomplishments they see that you value them, that you care about them. And in turn, they will give their all for you.

CHAPTER XI.

A LEADER IS FORGIVING, AND SEEKS FORGIVENESS

"The gentleman does not needlessly and unnecessarily remind an offender of a wrong he may have committed against him. He can not only forgive he can forget; and he strives for the nobleness of self and mildness of character which imparts sufficient strength to let the past be but the past. A true man of honor feels humbled himself when he cannot help humbling others." Robert E. Lee [269]

"Then came Peter to him and said, Lord how oft shall my brother sin against me, and I forgive him? Till seven times? Jesus saith to him, I say not unto thee, until seven times, but until seventy times seven." Matthew 18:21-22 [270]

In the last chapter we considered the leadership traits of justice and mercy. To not address the trait of forgiving is to fail to completely cover the traits needed in daily relations with others.

When we forgive we give a valuable member another chance. They failed, they likely learned from their failure. Giving them another chance enables us to use this now, wiser, and hence more valuable member. Who will likely be great at teaching others how to avoid making that same mistake benefiting our organization even more.

Notice, the leader does not ignore mistakes, does not allow subordinates to continue to make the same costly mistakes over and over. That is not forgiveness that is fear of accosting someone, fear of losing popularity over correction. The leader notices the mistake and values the mission and the subordinate enough to point it out and find a way to correct it so as to avoid it in the future.

Forgiveness also demonstrates to our team that we, the leaders, realize we all are human, and that they have value. It is easier to follow and give our all for a leader who cares enough to give us another chance. As in the quality of mercy it frees the one forgiven to go forth and try again.

"to whom little is forgiven, the same loveth little." Luke 7:47 [271]

One cannot be forgiven of a mistake made but that feelings of gratitude and affection spring up. The leader who forgives much is much loved. The real power of leaders is the love of their followers. When you see your leader as a kind and forgiving, loving parent, you will storm the gates of hell with a rock, attempt anything, and achieve much.

"Blessed is he whose transgression is forgiven, whose sin is covered... When I kept silence, my bones waxed old through my roaring all day long." Psalm 32:1, 3 [272]

When we ask forgiveness the burden of being found out, the fear of being passed over or let go disappears. Now all is out in the open. We demonstrate our honesty and integrity. When we receive forgiveness we are told that we have been given another chance. We are valued and now are once more part of the team, a stronger team for trust has been built.

It is also important for the leader to seek forgiveness. A manifestation of humility, when we seek forgiveness we are saying, "I made a mistake, I too am human. I am no better than you, and like you I need forgiveness. I am sorry.

Someone, I believe it was John Maxwell, once said that the words, I am sorry." Are some of the most powerful words in the human language. Think about it. They have the power to heal hurts, to reconcile, to enable friendship to recur. The power to take two people in opposition and unite them again in a common effort. They have the power to take two people who feel they have nothing in common and enable them to see that they are the same, both human, both able to make mistakes.

As a leader the ability to show your followers that you know that you are no better than they, to demonstrate that you value them enough to feel they deserve an apology and to ask that they forgive you, that ability is crucial to keep a team united. It is inspiring to see the effect on people. To see the awe on their faces come after hearing the leader say they are sorry, "I hope you'll forgive me." And very soon, on the heels of this awe, to see their faces break into smiles as they realize the significance of this. Our leader is showing us he or she is just like us, no better, no worse, and they want our forgiveness, they value us. We are a team. We can achieve anything now.

Of course, as in everything we have considered, if the apology is not sincere, if it is done merely to manipulate the followers, than very soon the followers understand that, and at that point the death of the team ensues. Leaders must be honest with their people, must trust them enough to be honest with them. Without trust there can be no team, no unity, no striving together for a common goal. And once the leader has the reputation of being a manipulator and insincere, their future as a leader is doomed.

"And be ye kind to one another, tender-hearted, forgiving one another, even as God for Christ's sake hath forgiven you." Ephesians 4:32 [273]

In reading Proverbs and in reading about Jackson I was surprised to see that King Solomon does not talk much on forgiveness or forgiving, and in reading of Jackson one is more impressed by the times he does not forgive than those he did.

In reading of Jackson one learns of his strained relations with his commanding officer while stationed with the federal army as a Major in

Florida, and of his disagreements with General Garnett and General Hill.

Jackson took serving his country very seriously. It was one of the core pillars of his life. His great importance he placed on this service made him very demanding and unforgiving at times. When subordinates failed to do what he would have done in their stead he could be very unforgiving. This is understandable, yet one initially feels almost embarrassed by his insufficient ability to forgive. Yet as we read more of Jackson we see he did have a great capacity for forgiving others.

See how moving and powerful is his demonstration of forgiveness. General Maxy Gregg had written some accusing statements regarding Jackson a few days before he himself was mortally wounded. Jackson visited General Gregg when he heard of his being injured.

Gregg sought to apologize for a discourteous endorsement he had written several days previously. Jackson had no recollection of the communiqué. His voice shaking with emotion, he took Gregg's hand and said, "The doctor tells me you have not long to live. Let me ask you to dismiss this matter from your mind and turn your thoughts to God and to the world to which you go." The Carolinian's eyes filled with tears, "I thank you, I thank you very much," he mumbled. Gregg would die twenty-four hours later. [274]

Jackson wrote in his maxims,

"Endeavor to be at peace with all men." [275]

Many authors point out Jackson's rigidness and seemingly inability to forgive. It is obvious on looking deeper that he was merciful and forgiving. However, people tend to remember hurts longer. All the more reason for we who want to be successful leaders to practice, and ask for, forgiveness. Forgiveness can have a tremendous impact on our team.

In researching this topic in the Bible I found very little in Proverbs on forgiveness, but much on it in other places. I believe that perhaps Solomon talked little about forgiveness because he had a hard time asking for forgiveness. I don't see him asking for forgiveness for his excessive focus on women and bowing to the desires of his wives and concubines over God's will. To ask forgiveness requires we first face up to making a mistake. Pride can prevent our ability to admit our mistakes and asking for forgiveness. Placing excessive importance on our mission can likewise inhibit our ability to be forgiving of others. We don't want to be too quick to forgive. We also don't want to be too proud to admit our mistakes. Both seldom result in correction of mistakes and improved performance.

Yet because forgiveness is so powerful we can't afford to not practice it. When we admit our own short-comings ask and forgiveness we put ourselves on the same level as our people, reaffirming to them that we don't see ourselves as so much more valuable than them. Our asking for forgiveness tells them we value them, quite a bit as it's hard to ask forgiveness. And, to give forgiveness to another who has made a mistake, gives them a second chance. It tells them we feel they are worth a second chance. They can learn from it and go on to excel. Both asking and granting forgiveness has a tremendous potential to build trust and unity, like nothing else, that will enable our team to overcome unbelievable challenges.

"It is the duty of nations as well as men to own their dependence upon the overruling power of God; to confess their sins and transgressions in humble sorrow, yet with assured hope that genuine repentance will lead to mercy and pardon..." Abraham Lincoln [276]

"God exalted Him to His right hand to be Prince and Leader and Savior and Deliverer and Preserver, in order to grant repentance to Israel and to bestow forgiveness and release from sins." Acts5:31 [277]

Lee, we have seen, was quick to forgive and saw the power in this. Jackson as well knew the power of seeking, receiving and granting forgiveness. Many leaders have seen the power of this. David is seen throughout the Bible to admit his shortcomings, seek forgiveness of God and others, and then give thanks for receiving forgiveness.

Jackson's, Lee's and my God places a great deal of importance on forgiveness. It brings his people back to Him allowing them to once more act as a unified team, and family. It was important enough for Him to go to great lengths to establish a system under Moses by which his people could be forgiven their sins. A foreshadowing of a greater means of forgiveness and reconciliation through His son. He seems to place unbelievable importance on this, enough to sacrifice His son to provide a means for our attaining forgiveness.

Remember what Christ said when his disciples asked, "But how many times do we have to forgive others?" "Seventy times seven times." was the answer. In other words, be generous with forgiving, and become a great leader.

CHAPTER XII.

A LEADER HAS INTEGRITY AND DOES WHAT IS RIGHT

It seems every book on leadership that lists the characteristics of a leader lists integrity. Few would argue that it is an indispensable trait. But what is integrity?

Integrity – "Soundness of moral character." Webster's Dictionary [278]

"In all things shewing thyself a pattern of good works: in doctrine shewing uncorruptness, gravity, sincerity, sound speech, that cannot be condemned;" Titus 2:7 [279]

Soundness of moral character, always doing what is right, consistently following the rules and laws laid down by a culture. Why is it so overwhelmingly agreed on as one of the core values a leader must possess?

In our last chapter we talked of how the act of confessing one's faults and admitting one's shortcomings is very powerful. It builds trust, and without trust there can be no unity, and without unity our efforts are weak and disjointed.

Isn't integrity after all just another way of saying being truthful, and trustworthy. Being the type of person who never violates God's laws and man's laws. If we are this type of person then those we work with never have to fear we will hurt them, lie, cheat, stab them in the back. They don't have to have one eye on the job and another covering their back. Trust frees us to work together as a team, holding nothing back.

I have worked for many organizations and in nearly every one I have been deceived, cheated and lied to. Being stabbed in the back in today's corporate world is more often the rule than the exception it once was. I remember entering into one venture saying to my wife, "I don't care if it is profitable, it will just be nice to work with a group of people I can trust. A team that I know will never stab me in the back." I have to say that it indeed has been the best thing I have ever undertaken and has not just resulted in success in that field, but has in fact spilled over into all my endeavors increasing my successes there as well. Integrity is powerful.

One leader I know talks of being transparent and its unmatched power. He feels it is one of the best predictors of a team's success. When people are willing to be transparent with one another, holding nothing back, admitting all their fears, foibles, and failures, an environment of trust is the result. Such honesty and openness breeds respect and caring for those who have sacrificed their image to reveal their true selves; who have risked embarrassment and ridicule to gain the confidence of others. The trust thus

generated enables a group of people to become a unified, focused force to

be reckoned with. Each one works with and for the others, never needing to

look back, never holding back. One for all and all for one.

King David was a man of integrity. He wasn't perfect, but he was open

and transparent when he made a mistake.

"And if thou wilt walk before me, as David thy father walked, in integrity of heart, and in uprightness, to do according to all that I have commanded thee, and wilt keep my statutes and my judgments: Then I will establish the throne of thy kingdom upon Israel forever…" 1 Kings 9:4-5 [280]

"I know also, my God, that thou triest the heart, and hast pleasure in uprightness." 1 Chronicles 29:17 [281]

"He chose David also his servant, and took him from the sheepfolds: From following the ewes great with young he brought him to feed Jacob his people, and Israel his inheritance. So he fed them according to the integrity of his heart; and guided them by the skillfulness of his hands." Psalm 78:70-72 [282]

When the heat is on, when the pressure mounts, one's lack of integrity

will be seen. It is then that he or she, who is the most honest triumphs.

"He that walketh uprightly walketh surely: but he that perverteth his ways shall be known." Proverbs 10:9 [283]

"The integrity of the upright shall guide them: but the perverseness of transgressors shall destroy them." Proverbs 11:3 [284]

"Righteousness keepeth him that is upright in the way: but wickedness overthroweth the sinner." Proverbs 13:6 [285]

Did our role model, Thomas Stonewall Jackson have integrity? Grant said of Jackson that he,

"was the most honest human being I ever knew." JIRp35 [286]

His surgeon, Dr Hunter McGuire said of him,

"Under every and all circumstances he never forgot that he was a Christian and acted up to his Christian faith unswervingly." SHp30 [287]

Did our mentor, Thomas Jackson feel integrity was important? What were his views? His views on it were recorded by many people.

"Rather than violate the known will of God, I would forfeit my life." JIRp91 [288]

"Whilst we attach so much importance to being free from temporal bondage, we much attach far more to being free from the bondage of sin." [289]

His friend, minister, and chief of staff, the Reverend R. L. Dabney says of him,

"He spoke emphatically of the duty of conforming our wills to God's, and of a thoroughly cheerful acquiescence whenever His will was manifested... His favorite maxim was: "Duty is ours: consequences are God's." He spoke much of the blessedness of a full and hearty obedience, in its effects upon the Christian's own happiness." [290]

And the one who knew him best says this,

It was a continued delight to him to dwell upon the blessedness of perfect acquiescence in the Divine will." [291]

Thomas Jackson found true happiness in obeying God's laws in all things. He was transparent as he shared his love for his wife in his letters to her. He again was transparent as he shared his beliefs with his staff and others, and as he prayed at campfire and in battle, openly, for his men. His honesty and Christian values gave his men the ability to trust in him completely, even when they had no idea where he was leading them, nor into what. As Hugh White, a private in the 4th Virginia Regiment, Stonewall Brigade said,

My dear father:
I do not think that any man can take General Jackson's place in the confidence and love of his troops. I wish I could go with him, though my hardships would be more than doubled. I have learned to look up to him with implicit confidence, and to approach him with perfect freedom...[292]

He became General Robert E. Lee's most trusted lieutenant as he strove to serve his commander without a hidden agenda. When their opinions diverged, general Jackson trusted in his commander completely and so was an instrument that could be used with utmost effect. As Lee said of Jackson when he was mortally wounded,

"He has lost his left arm; but I have lost my right arm." [293]

If we then are honest and open in our relationships with our family, friends, and team; and if we can, without fear, be honest in our relationship with God; then we too can be effective leaders. When we practice integrity, doing what is right, being morally above reproach, being transparent, then the trust gained enables the entire team to operate as one unified, powerful, unstoppable force. Able to overcome impossible odds and attain victory in our endeavors.

CHAPTER XIII.
A LEADER ONLY SPEAKS POSITIVE

"A gentle tongue [with its healing power] is a tree of life, but willful contrariness in it breaks down the spirit" Proverbs 15:4 [294]

"A merry heart maketh a cheerful countenance: but by sorrow of the heart the spirit is broken." Proverbs 15:13 [295]

"The lips of the righteous feed many: but fools die for want of wisdom." Proverbs 10:21 [296]

"The wise in heart shall be called prudent: and the sweetness of the lips increaseth learning." Proverbs 16:21 [297]

Many of the books I have read over the last 40 plus years on leadership have stressed the importance of concentrating on positive. When one attains and maintains a positive mental attitude, one constantly has the energy, and optimism, to strive to achieve, and to encourage others to do their best at the same time.

When in my twenties, thanks to my mother, I began reading guideposts magazine and the writings of Dr. Norman Vincent Peale. My entire outlook was changed from one of defeat and inadequacy, to one of "I can, I will." To this day I recommend his books and those of Napoleon Hill and Zig Ziglar to other young leaders, and to those not so young as well.

Jackson planned for the negative, but then focused on the positive. It seems that no matter how great the odds against him, he would look at all factors, plan for victory, and then refuse to accept anything else as possible.

> *"Jackson repeatedly told his soldiers,*
> *'Never take counsel of your fears.'"* [298]

This quote was one of general George S. Patton's favorites. In fact I have been impressed by the similarities in these two leaders and am myself convinced that Jackson had a profound influence on General Patton's life, views, and combat tactics.

When one concentrates on the negative, it saps one's will, one's belief that he or she can overcome. It is like adding an 80 pound pack onto our shoulders while we're going up a hill. Negative thoughts weigh our spirit down. In the 1970's the idea of the "self-fulfilling prophecy" was born. If we say to ourselves, "I can't do it." "I'm sure to fail." We usually do. If on the other hand we use positive self-talk, such as Shad Helmstetter, in his books and lectures proposes then we can talk ourselves into succeeding, growing and achieving. Like the little engine who said over and over, "I think I can, I think I can."

It becomes obvious if one reads of Jackson that he was a positive thinker,

"What I willed to do, I could do." [299]

who in turn helped others to adopt a positive outlook. His faith in God and the Bible fostered this.

Robertson reveals, based on looking at Jackson's personal Bible, that Jackson's two favorite Bible verses appear to have been:

Revelation 21:4 "And God shall wipe away all tears from their eyes; and there shall be no more death, neither sorrow, nor crying, neither shall there be any more pain: for the former things are passed away." However the verse that most inspired him was Romans 8:28: "And we know that all things work together for good to them that love God, to them that are called according to his purpose." [300]

James I. Robertson Jr, who has written quite possibly the most thorough and best biography of Jackson, accurately surmises the source of his positiveness.

"Jackson was optimistic because he had faith." [301]

"We are all children of this world...Amid affliction let us hope for happiness...However dark the night, I am cheered with an anticipated glorious and luminous morrow...No earthly calamity can shake my hope in the future so long as God is my friend." [302]

Thomas Jackson strove himself to keep his focus on the positive and when tempted to grumble, he would again turn to the source of his guidance and inspiration, and regain his focus.

"My darling wife, I am just overburdened with work, I hope you will not think hard at receiving only very short letters from your loving husband. A number of officers are with me, but people keep coming to my tent-though let me say no more. A Christian should never complain. The Apostle Paul said, 'I glory in tribulations.' What a bright example for others." [303]

"Nor discontentedly complain as some of them did-"
1 Corinthians 10:10 [304]

When wounded he was heard by Captain James Power Smith to say,

"Many would regard [these injuries] as a great misfortune; I regard them as one of the blessings of my life." "All things work together for good to them that love God." Smith quoted. "Yes, that's it, that's it. [305]

Someone once said, One cannot be sad who himself brings cheer to others. I believe that this was true of Jackson. He sought to raise up all those around him who despaired. When his wife became discouraged during an illness he wrote her,

You must not be discouraged by the slowness of recovery. Look up to Him who giveth liberally for faith to be resigned to His will. And trust Him for that measure of health which will most glorify Him and advance to the greatest extent your own real happiness. We are sometimes suffered to be in a state of perplexity, that our faith may be tried and grow stronger. All things work together for good to God's children." [306]

Try to look up and be cheerful, and not desponding. Trust your kind Heavenly Father, and by the eye of faith see that all things with you are right and for your best interest. The clouds come, pass over us, and are followed by bright sunshine; so, in God's moral dealings with us, He permits us to have trouble awhile. But let us, even in the most trying dispensations of His providence, be cheered by the brightness which is a little ahead. Try to live near to Jesus, and secure that peace which flows like a river." [307]

Jackson constantly focused on his faith, on God's love for him, and the hope of eternal life in heaven. He also used another powerful method of staying focused on the positive, thanksgiving.

"I am so thankful to our ever-kind Heavenly Father for having so improved my eyes as to enable me to write at night. He continually showers blessings upon me." [308]

There is a strong, positive power in giving thanks. Years ago I found that one way to ever keep a positive attitude for those around me, even during times that were less than uplifting, was to find 100 reasons to thank God. Don't get me wrong and assume I find one hundred grandiose things to be thankful for. Not all of the things I am thankful for are big things. "I thank you Father for: My wife, our children, my country and its freedoms, the work you have given me to do, for...onions, tomatoes, jalipeno peppers, guitar music, flowers, cookies, dogs, babies, Generals Lee and Jackson, friends, comedy, Saturdays, the snooze alarm, COFFEE, ..." Try it and see. After 100 thank you's, it's hard to focus on negatives.

Read works by positive thinkers. Speak positive and confidence. Count your blessings and be thankful. And, become one who is able to overcome challenges by the extra power that comes from a positive outlook. Then see

how your positive focus encourages and energizes all those around you.

Become more like Jackson who said,

"Nothing earthly can ever mar my happiness. I know that heaven is in store for me." [309]

CHAPTER XIV.

A LEADER COMMUNICATES WISELY – CONTROLS HIS MOUTH AND EMOTIONS.

"He that is slow to anger is better than the mighty, and he that ruleth his spirit than he that taketh a city." Proverbs 16:32 [310]

"Who so keepeth his mouth and his tongue keepeth his soul from troubles." Proverbs 21:23 [311]

A leader displays many traits. We have looked at the need to seek counsel, to accept discipline, to plan well, and to be humble and reverent. We have examined being just and impartial and how this involves knowing when and how to discipline and award credit and praise. Being a servant-leader has been considered. We have pondered the power of positive.

Many of these traits involve communication. The ability to take in information and advice is important. We can't do this, we can't listen well, if we are too busy talking. Both talking and listening are critically important, as is how well we do both.

Many have said there is a reason we have two ears and one mouth. That listening is more important and that we should do twice as much listening as we do talking. Several respected leaders have stated that if we would be a good conversationalist, all we need do is to get the other person to talk about themselves and listen well to them. To be still and to listen enables us to learn and may prevent us from revealing more than is wise. Also it minimizes our chances of offending another.

"Even a fool, when he holdeth his peace, is counted wise: and he that shutteth his lips is esteemed a man of understanding." *Proverbs 17:28* [312]

Most of us have a difficult time using our ears and tongue properly and well, and none of us are able to do it 100% of the time.

I believe the ability to ask questions, and then listen to the answers can make a significant difference in ones career. If you don't ask questions and listen, you can't gain the insight needed to excel. And, asking questions demonstrates humility, confidence, and a desire to excel. However, as mentioned in Chapter III., discernment is important. It is a good idea to know, or at least have a fair idea, if the person will see the opportunity to help you, or to try to use it to convince others that you are incompetent. If you are surrounded by back stabbers, go somewhere else, lest in time you become one. If you're not sure, it's better to venture and to question than to delay self-growth out of fear of criticism.

I have always been a question asker. (I might add, it's always important to listen well enough to not ask questions when that subject was just addressed.) In every position I have been in I have rapidly advanced, been seen as a person of integrity and competence, who could be trusted. I also found that my subordinates were more willing to ask questions of me for they knew I did and would not think badly of them. Because they weren't afraid to ask for information they have grown faster, advanced sooner, and I and my organization benefited from that faster growth.

A successful leader IS a servant. Part of being a servant involves being able to gather data on what those served need. You can only learn this if you truly care and are willing to seek the answers. You may have to learn it by observing. Nothing is better than time spent in the trenches with your people. It is in the trenches that you really see and experience their needs.

A president of a company once complained to my father that despite raises his people didn't like him. When he asked why my father said, "Because they don't think you care." The president was highly insulted, and I think, stung by knowing, on reflection, that it was true. My father suggested that it would do more good to just walk through the plant each day and stop now and again and say hello to employees. This man tried it and was shocked to see that, far more than benefits and monetary rewards, his walking among the people and appearing to care, resulted in far more productivity and profit. He began to enjoy it and came to truly care about his people, and was a far happier man.

"A wise man will hear, and will increase learning;
and a man of understanding shall attain unto wise counsels." Proverbs
1:5 [313]

"The way of a fool is right in his own eyes: but he that hearkeneth unto
counsel is wise." Proverbs 12:15 [314]

"He that hath understanding spareth his words:
and a man of understanding is of an excellent spirit." Proverbs 17:27 [315]

When another speaks, listen to their words, their voice, and observe their non-verbal communication. Come to understand and value their feelings and opinions. Then you'll gain greater insight, respond more effectively, and you then are more likely to gain their respect, trust, and cooperation.

"Bow down thine ear, and hear the words of the wise, and apply thine
heart unto my knowledge." Proverbs 22:17 [316]

As General Jackson wrote in his book of maxims,

"Attend to a person who is addressing you." [317]

And as Dr Dabney found him to be,

"equally considerate of the taste and character of those with whom he held intercourse. He molded his share of that intercourse accordingly. His scrupulous and delicate politeness made it always his aim to render others easy and comfortable in his presence." [318]

So in summary, listen first, listen as you interact, and then listen to learn what effect your intervention had.

Thomas Jackson was a good listener. He listened to Robert E. Lee. He trusted his leader and acted to carry out the mission. When he was wounded Lee wrote him saying, "You have lost your left arm but I have lost my right." Because he obeyed, he was like an extension of Lee. Lee never had to guess what he would do or if he would do it. Trusting in his following orders Lee could then focus on other fronts. Jackson listened.

General James Longstreet seemed to usually propose other options and in some instances appears to have disregarded orders, failing to obey them. The difference can be seen in the results. Many knowledgeable men feel that had General Jackson been present at Gettysburg the confederates would have gained the high ground and this battle would have been a confederate victory. As it was, it became a defeat, and many blame it on Longstreet for delaying so long to obey orders.

Appreciate the importance of being a good listener and encourage your people to be good listeners by your example.

Listening enables one to learn necessary information, to obtain advice on how to best use that information, and after acting allows one to evaluate that action's effectiveness. Eyes may be better at times but when one is able to listen to one's observers then one has the advantage of, "many sets of eyes".

> *"He that answereth a matter before he heareth it,*
> *it is folly and shame unto him." Proverbs 18:13* [319]

> *"The words of a man's mouth are as deep as waters,*
> *and the wellspring of wisdom as a flowing brook." Proverbs 18:4* [320]

Again, listen to more than just the facts, listen to the feelings and understand others' hearts. Listening allows us to navigate these waters safely with our eyes open, and to listen to hear any sound of an "approaching waterfall" and thus avoid mishap.

We mentioned that some feel we have two ears and one mouth for a good reason. The reason being that listening is twice as important. After all we learn by listening not talking. But perhaps there is another reason. It's hard to get in trouble by listening. In fact using our ears and listening conveys valuing the person speaking and is therapeutic and establishes a bond. It's far more often that our mouths get us in trouble. So, maybe we have two ears but only one mouth because the mouth is twice as dangerous and hard to control. Both Solomon and James talk about this a lot.

"A fool's lips enter into contention, and his mouth calleth for strokes. A fool's mouth is his destruction, and his lips are the snare of his soul. The words of a talebearer are as wounds, and they go down into the innermost parts of the belly." Proverbs 18:6-8 [321]

"Death and life are in the power of the tongue: and they that love it shall eat the fruit thereof." Proverbs 18:21 [322]

"...he that speaketh lies shall not escape. ...he that speaketh lies shall perish." Proverbs 19:5, 9 [323]

"Whoso keepeth his mouth and his tongue keepeth his soul from troubles." Proverbs 21:23 [324]

"For in many ways we offend all. If any man offend not in word, the same is a perfect man, and able also to bridle the whole body. Behold, we put bits in the horses' mouths, that may obey us; and we turn about their whole body. Behold also the ships, which though they be so great, and are driven of fierce winds, yet are they turned about with a very small helm, whithersoever the governor listeth. Even so the tongue is a little member, and boasteth great things. Behold how great a master a little fire kindleth! And the tongue is a fire, a world of iniquity; so is the tongue among our members, that it defileth the whole body, and setteth on fire the course of nature; and it is set on fire of hell. For every kind of beasts, and of birds, and of serpents, and of things in the sea, is tamed, and hath been tamed of mankind: but the tongue can no man tame; it is an unruly evil, full of deadly poison. Therefore bless we God, even the Father; and therewith curse we men, which are made after the similitude of God. Out of the same mouth proceedeth blessing and cursing. My brethren these things ought not so to be." James 3:2-10 [325]

Who is a wise man and endued with knowledge among you? Let him show out of a good conversation his works with meekness of wisdom."
James 3:13 [326]

When we choose to exercise our oral muscle, it is best to concentrate and avoid three harmful things, and to strive to do two others. Avoid:

1) Hurting others via destructive criticism.

2) Discouraging others through negative talk.

3) Saying things best kept a secret.

In this way we can avoid harming our associates, our clients, our mission and ourselves.

We should strive to use the tongue to accomplish positive by: 1) telling the truth, providing accurate information; and 2) encouraging our associates and clients.

The tongue is a sharp and powerful tool.

"There is that speaketh like the piercings of a sword: but the tongue of the wise is health." *Proverbs 12:18* [327]

"A fool's mouth is his destruction, and his lips are the snare of his soul."
Proverbs 18:7 [328]

It can harm others...

"The words of a talebearer are as wounds,
and they go down into the innermost parts of the belly." Proverbs 18:8 [329]

"A brother offended is harder to be won than a strong city:
and their contentions are like the bars of a castle." Proverbs 18:19 [330]

And, it can harm us...

"Seest thou a man that is hasty in his words?
There is more hope of a fool than of him." Proverbs 29:20 [331]

The tongue is necessary to correct errors in thinking or acting. But the

control of it, of the temper, is necessary to avoid more harm than good.

"He is in the way of life that keepeth instruction: but he that refuseth
reproof erreth. He that hideth hatred with lying lips, and he that uttereth
a slander, is a fool. In the multitude of words there wanteth not sin: but he
that refraineth his lips is wise. The tongue of the wise is as choice silver:
the heart of the wicked is little worth. The lips of the righteous feed many:
but fools die for want of wisdom." Proverbs 10:17 [332]

"A soft answer turneth away wrath: but grievous words stir up anger."
Proverbs 15:1 [333]

"The discretion of a man deferreth his anger; and it is his glory to pass
over a transgression." Proverbs 19:11 [334]

"It is an honor for a man to cease from strife: but every fool will be
meddling." Proverbs 20:3 [335]

"Jackson's friend the Reverend James R. Graham, considered 'marvelous
self-control' to be one of Jackson's strongest qualities... 'He that is slow to
anger is better than the mighty, and he that ruleth his spirit than he that
taketh a city.' Proverbs 16:32" [336]

*"A fool uttereth all in his mind: but a wise man keepeth it in til afterwards.
Proverbs 29:11,20 [337]*

In addition to what we have considered thus far, there is another issue addressed by many leaders of the past, and that is the use of profane language or cursing. Foul language never is a good decision. Of Jackson it was said,

"He would not brook courseness or vulgarity." [338]

Like Grant he no doubt felt it a form of weakness, and an imposition on others' sensibilities.

Jackson wrote in his book of maxims,

"Endeavor to be at peace with all men." [339]

We need to be aware of how much any negative words can result in the discouragement of others. A leader cannot afford to speak any words without first weighing their effect on his associates. As mentioned in other chapters, Jackson tended to be an encourager, not a discourager and perhaps this is why friends, family and subordinates were able to overcome otherwise challenging trials.

A successful leader uses care to avoid divulging things that may hurt others or their mission. It is important to keep secrets secret. If one can't be trusted to keep a secret, one can't be trusted. And, without trust there can be neither relationship nor the resulting synergy that always results in more than what one can accomplish alone. Trust is the glue that unites a team, enlists their support, and concentrates all efforts. Without trust no one will follow, and as John Maxwell has said, "if you start out and no one follows you're not leading, you're just out for a walk."

"A prudent man concealeth knowledge:
but the heart of fools proclaimeth foolishness." Proverbs 12:23 [340]

"He that keepeth his mouth keepeth his life:
but he that openeth wide his lips shall have destruction."
Proverbs 13:3 [341]

"The tongue of the wise useth knowledge aright:
but the mouth of fools poureth out foolishness." Proverbs 15:2 [342]

"A fool's mouth if his destruction, and his lips are the snare of his soul."
Proverbs 18:7 [343]

"Debate thy cause with thy neighbor himself:
and discover not a secret to another." Proverbs 25:9 [344]

Jackson was concerned about giving away plans and so impairing his chances of surprising the enemy and attaining success. Divulging military secrets can result in losing the lives of your men. "Loose lips sink ships." Reading of him one is struck by his appreciation of the value of secrecy and the unbelievable lengths he took to keep word from getting out regarding his plans. As Jackson was wont to say,

"Always mystify, mislead and surprise the enemy if possible." [345]

We have looked long and hard at how the tongue can be destructive.

Let us look a bit more on how it can do good. The tongue can so inspire

and encourage others. When a leader speaks of his caring and shares his

oneness with his people from his heart, it can result in a bond strong enough

to withstand, and overcome, all that lies before them.

"The lips of the righteous feed many:
but fools die for want of wisdom." Proverbs 10:21 [346]

"Pleasant words are as a honeycomb, sweet to the soul,
and health to the bones." Proverbs 16:24 [347]

At first Manassas after a Union bombardment left 27 injured or dead
what calmed his men was Jackson who rode back and forth along the line
moving "about in that shower of death as calmly as a farmer about his
farm when the seasons are good."...Another noted that a glance revealed,
"The trust in God, and utter reliance on His will were surely there- but no
apathetic calmness. The blaze of the eye was unmistakable- there plainly
was a soul on fire with deep feeling, and the ardor of battle...A slumbering
volcano clearly burned beneath that face so calm and collected." An aura
of confidence seemed to surround him. So did Jackson's quiet words:
Steady, men, steady! All's well." He offered those reassurances despite
the fact that he had been painfully wounded. [348]

At one point during the battle of Slaughter mountain there was a moment
when the men were confused and on the verge of falling back. Captain
Charles Minor Blackford writes of Jackson, As he got amongst the
disordered troops he drew his sword and then reached over and took his
battle flag from my man, Bob Isbell, who was carrying it, and dropping

his bridal rein, waved it over his head, and at the same time cried out in a loud voice: "Rally, men! Remember Winder! Where's my Stonewall Brigade! Forward men! Forward!" As he did so he dashed to the front, and our men followed with a yell and drove everything before them. [349]

A confident, positive leader is a tremendous force for success.

We all need encouragement. However, expressions of caring only work when they are meant, and come from the heart of a leader who really cares.

"There is gold, and a multitude of rubies:
but the lips of knowledge are a precious jewel." Proverbs 20:15 [350]

In this letter Jackson encourages his wife,

"You must not be discouraged at the slowness of recovery. Look up to Him who giveth liberally for faith to be resigned to His divine will. And trust Him for that measure of health which will most glorify Him and advance to the greatest extent your own real happiness. We are sometimes suffered to be in a state of perplexity, that our faith may be tried and grow stronger. All things work together for good to God's children." [351]

"For these great and signal victories our sincere and humble thanks are due unto Almighty God. We should in all things acknowledge the hand of Him who reigns in heaven and rules among the armies of men...We can but express the grateful conviction of our mind that God was with us and gave us the victory, and unto His name be the praise." [352]

The tongue, a force for good and evil. Much depends on whether it speaks the truth or a lie.

"The lips of truth shall be established forever:

but a lying tongue is but for a moment...Lying lips are abomination to the Lord:
but they that deal truly are his delight." Proverbs 12:19,22 [353]

"A false witness shall not go unpunished, and he that speaketh lies shall not escape...A false witness shall not be unpunished, and he that speaketh lies shall perish." Proverbs 19:5,9 [354]

We all need honest, sincere, encouragement.

Finally, it's important to realize that we are best equipped to comfort others when we ourselves have experienced hurt and the solace of others and our God.

"Who comforteth in all our tribulation, that we may be able to comfort them which are in any trouble, by the comfort wherewith we ourselves are comforted of God." 2 Cor 1:4 [355]

Once hurt we better understand its pain, and the value of consolation. The more we are able to use it in turn to help others.

Notice that in the previous scene Jackson went before them. As Grant said of another in praising him, "with him it was always come, not go." A leader leads. As James Longstreet, Grant's best man at his wedding, and one of Robert E. Lee's generals, is purported to have said, "You can't lead from behind."

"At Chancellorsville: Close to the front he had ridden; again and again he had shouted, "Press on, press on!" The ecstasy of conflict appeared to have seized him. Never had he been so transformed- never in such sure

reliance upon the God of battle. Every time the wild yell of victory swept across the fields or through the wood, he would lift his head and give thanks. He did also, what he had never been seen to do before in action. If he passed a spot where some of his men lay dead, their blood still wet and red, he would draw in the sorrel and raise his hand as if he were a priestly crusader who prayed for the souls of the fallen and blessed them for their valor." [356]

A leader sees the need for encouragement and inspiration. He or she then steps forward to both speak and act. Realize that, action speaks louder than words.

Lastly, Let us not overlook the ability of interjecting tasteful humor as a means of relieving tension and lifting spirits.

"Heaviness in the heart of man maketh it stoop: but a good word maketh it glad." Proverbs 12:25 [357]

"A merry heart maketh a cheerful countenance: but by sorrow of the heart the spirit is broken." Proverbs 15:13 [358]

" A merry heart doeth much good." Proverbs 17:21-23. Though not particularly known for a great sense of humor he did attempt to jest with general Jeb Stuart. "Howdy do, general. Get off and tell us about your trip. They tell me that from the time you crossed the Potomac until you got back again you didn't sing a song or crack a joke, but as soon as you got on Virginia soil you began to whistle, "Home, Sweet Home." [359]

One final thought. We have seen how destructive the tongue can be if not controlled. Any gun safety course teaches, not to mix guns and alcohol. At times I think that the tongue is a far more dangerous weapon. The use of alcohol dramatically impairs our ability to control the tongue, perhaps that is why Lee and Jackson abstained from its use.

CHAPTER XV.

A LEADER IS KIND, MERCIFUL, FAITHFUL, LOYAL.

"And they spake unto him saying, If thou be kind to this people, and please them, and speak good words to them, they will be thy servants forever." 2 Chronicles 10:7 [360]

Having studied the lives of Lee and Jackson one would almost believe this is being spoken by them to you, or by Ezra to you.

If you are sincerely kind and caring, and value others, they will sense this; however, if you only pretend to in order to manipulate others, they will discern this as well.

"Whoso walketh uprightly shall be saved: but he that is perverse in his ways shall fall at once." Proverbs 28:18 [361]

"Let not mercy and truth forsake thee: bind them about thine neck; write them upon the table of thine heart." Proverbs 3:3-4 [362]

These words in King Solomon's book of proverbs sum up the importance of showing your people kindness and mercy; and of being faithful and loyal to them. The leader who treats his people this way will be rewarded by their loyalty and faithfulness, and by their doing the impossible for him or her. We see this borne out in the lives of Lee, Jackson, and Patton, and by their interest in their people.

Having become familiar with Thomas Jonathan Jackson, one can almost hear him say them, echoing King Solomon.

"Withhold not good from them to whom it is due, when it is in the power of thine hand to do it." Proverbs 3:27-28 [363]

Along with kindness mercy also shows caring, understanding, and respect. Again when one shows these traits to ones people, they in turn show them back to you as their leader.

"Do they not err that devise evil? But mercy and truth shall be to them that devise good." Proverbs 14:22 [364]

What is mercy? In writing this book I often consulted Webster's dictionary. But, I believe I found the best definition in a Bible commentary. James Vernon McGee in his commentary on Proverbs says this of mercy,

"Mercy is loving-kindness. The law was given by Moses, but grace and truth came by Jesus Christ. What is loving-kindness? It is grace; it is more than kindness. The teacher asked a little girl the difference between kindness and loving-kindness. The little girl answered, "well, if you go in and ask your mama for a piece of bread with some butter on it, and she gives it to you, that's kindness. But if she puts a little jam on it without your asking her, that is loving-kindness." My friend, God puts a little jam on it for us-loving-kindness and truth, let these not forsake thee: bind them about thine neck; write them upon the table of thine heart." [365]

How could that fail to win the hearts and loyalty of the recipients.

Let's look further at the type of person who shows mercy, and the effects of showing mercy to others.

"A righteous man regardeth the life of his beast: but the tender mercies of the wicked are cruel." Proverbs 12:10 [366]

"The merciful man doeth good to his own soul: but he that is cruel troubleth his own flesh." Proverbs 11:17 [367]

"He that despiseth his neighbor sinneth: but he that hath mercy on the poor, happy is he." Proverbs 14:21 [368]

It has been said that Rockefeller was a hard businessman. When his health failed his Dr. prescribed being kind to others and through this he found true happiness, health and a long and successful life.

"Mercy and truth preserve the king: and his throne is upholden by mercy." Proverbs 20:28 [369]

All good and great people care about the needs of others. They focus on others rather than on themselves. As a twenty year old I was sad and lonely. I learned that when I took my eyes off myself and focused on others, I soon forgot my problems and found happiness through helping them.

"He that hath pity upon the poor lendeth to the Lord: and that which he hath given will he pay him again." Proverbs 19:17 [370]

"He that hath a bountiful eye shall be blessed; for he giveth his bread to the poor." Proverbs 22:9 [371]

Those who have a bountiful eye, who show loving kindness, heaping over service to their people shall be blessed, with trust, loyalty and even more. Lee's men, after he surrendered to Grant, told him they still loved him. In reading great leaders lives examples abound of their men showing them acts of love and loyalty throughout their lives.

Leaders show caring in a variety of ways. Great, successful leaders always truly care for their people. Sincere caring leads the leader to think about his or her people. What do they need at this moment? What can I do for them? Venturing out amongst one's people, caring enough to learn first hand their needs is extremely valuable. Having discovered these one must then specifically address these issues and meet these needs.

Meeting their needs is probably the most telling and has the greatest impact. But a kind word, a cherry disposition, sharing a positive outlook, all can be as a balm on a sore and many times is just what the Dr. would order.

"All the days of the afflicted are evil: but he that is of a merry heart hath a continual feast." Proverbs 15:15 [372]

"Better is a dinner of herbs where love is, then a stalled(fattened) ox and hatred therewith." Proverbs 15:17 [373]

Understanding another's hurts and offering words of caring and consolation as discussed in the preceding chapter also demonstrates caring and this is not missed by those receiving it. Jackson's caring was not missed by those around him. As Jackson's wife said,

> *"The overflowing sunshine of his heart was a reflection from the Sun of Righteousness, and he always said we could not love an earthly creature too much if we only loved God more."* [374]

Sincere caring for others is evident to those close to the leader; and serves as an example to them.

Jackson's wife stated,

> *"His heart was as soft as a woman's; he was full of love and gentleness."* [375]

When you've done all you can for your people, you can always take their needs to God as well, praying and interceding on their behalf. In a letter to his wife Jackson wrote,

> *" What a consoling thought it is, to know that we may, with perfect confidence, commit all our friends in Jesus to the care of our Heavenly Father, with an assurance that all shall be well with them."* [376]

At times it is we who must console others, especially in times of great loss.

Jackson wrote Colonel Frederick Holliday of the loss of two men,

> *"Their deaths comported well with their patriotic devotion to our cause. Their names should be held in gratified remembrance by us who have been privileged survivors, and by all who admire patriotic devotion to civil and religious liberty. I have reason to believe that both of them have entered into that rest which remaineth for the people of God."* [377]

At the battle of Cold Harbor when urged by Major Roberdeau Wheat not to expose himself unnecessarily Jackson replied,

"I will try and not go into danger, unnecessarily. But Major you will be in danger greater than I, and I hope you will not get hurt. Each of us has his duty to perform, without regard to consequences; we must perform it and trust to providence." [378]

The consequences of sincere caring are powerful. How would you feel if a boss expressed concern for you, such as, "Be careful driving. You're valuable to us."

Agreeing with another may be a means of displaying kindness, respect and loyalty. Conversely, at times what one needs most is not agreeing, but loving disagreement, constructive criticism, caring rebuke.

"Open rebuke is better than secret love. Faithful are the wounds of a friend, but the kisses of an enemy are deceitful." Proverbs 27:5-6 [379]

Objective, constructive criticism, spoken never in anger, always out of wanting what is best for another leads one to the right kind of rebuke. In his book of maxims Jackson writes,

"Do not suffer your feelings to betray you into too much vehemence or earnestness or to being overbearing." [380]

Jackson's wife said of him,

"He was utterly free from censoriousness, envy, detraction, and all uncharitableness, and certainly kept his rule that if he could not say something good of a man, he would not speak of him at all." [381]

In this way good always is the result.

"Iron sharpeneth iron: so a man sharpeneth the countenance of a friend."
Proverbs 27:17 [382]

When people are always honest with one another, they come to see both rebuke and praise objectively, and are hurt by neither.

"As the refining pot for silver, and the furnace for gold;
so is a man to his praise." Proverbs 27:21 [383]

Again, consistently looking for your peoples' needs and putting them first likely demonstrates faithfulness and loyalty best. Honest caring and striving to help their growth is not missed

"That which is desired in a man is loyalty and kindness and his glory and delight are his giving, but a poor man is better than a liar."
Proverbs 19:22 [384]

"I am the good shepherd: the good shepherd giveth his life for the sheep."
Jn 10:11 [385]

Jackson's caring was not missed by those around him. The reverend William Hoge reports of Jackson,

"How anxious he was for his army!" [386]

Private Hugh White said of Jackson,

"I have learned to look up to him with implicit confidence, and to approach him with perfect freedom, being always assured of a kind and attentive hearing..." [387]

In conclusion, a leader likely best shows his or her caring by demonstrating the fact they are constantly thinking of what their people need, and persistently striving to meet these needs. Both Thomas Jackson, and General Robert E. Lee displayed these traits and are good examples of these and the results that may be attained by those who likewise show their caring.

J. Steven Wilkins, in his book Call of Duty, notes several scenarios in General Lee's life that paint a picture the power of showing kindness, loyalty, and faithfulness to ones subordinates and the result of such behavior when adopted by leaders.

"Lee's kindness was not that forced, artificial sort one often sees in people who believe their reputation depends upon how nice they appear to be before others. Rather it was the natural outflow of the heart of a man who sought constantly to esteem others better than himself." [388]

"After the war a friend asked General Lee why he did not make his escape before the surrender, when that course was open to him. Lee responded that he was unwilling to separate his fate from that of the men who had fought under him for so long. This answer is the key to the loyalty Lee inspired in his men. He truly loved them. Indeed, the respect Lee enjoyed in their eyes was only rivaled by the respect he himself had for them. The men were his chief pride and his first obligation. As long as he lived Lee

considered those he served in the Southern Army as the most honorable of men." [389]

"Lee was always careful to show many small kindnesses to his officers...Not just officers but common soldiers were always given great consideration." [390]

"His letters are filled with expressions of concern for his soldiers. He regularly wrote to president Davis reporting shortages of food, clothing, shoes, and other provisions. His efforts on their behalf were untiring." [391]

General Robert E.Lee wrote in a letter to his wife,

" It is raining heavily. The men are all exposed on the mountain, with the enemy opposite to us. We are without tents and for two nights I have lain buttoned up in my overcoat. To-day my tent came up and I am in it. Yet I fear I shall not sleep for thinking of the poor men." [392]

In his book about his father, the son, Captain Robert E. Lee quotes from

General Long,

" "No commander was ever more careful, and never had care for the comfort of an army given rise to greater devotion. He was constantly calling the attention of the authorities to the wants of his soldiers, making every effort to provide them with food and clothing. The feeling for him was one of love, not of awe or dread. They could approach him with the assurance that they would be received with kindness and consideration, and that any just complaint would receive proper attention. There was no condescension in his manner, but he was ever simple, kind, and sympathetic, and his men, while having unbounded faith in him as a leader, almost worshipped him as a man. These relations of affection and mutual confidence between the army and its commander had much to do with the undaunted bravery displayed by the men, and bore a due share in the many victories they gained." [393]

How wonderful if similar things will be said of us in the future. Rest assured if it is you will have accomplished great things with your people. Better than a monument of stone or bronze is the memory of your sincere, humble, caring and the effect it continues to have on those who continue on after you.

CHAPTER XVI.
A LEADER IS DILIGENT

We have looked at the importance of gathering good information, seeking wise counsel, coming to a decision, making plans and now we will discuss taking action.

A successful leader will not be lazy, indifferent or careless. He or she will take all into consideration especially what the challenges are and what resources we have to meet these demands. We will discuss the wise use of resources in the next chapter. A successful leader will be painstaking, persistent and industrious. The leader who is seen by his superiors and peers and subordinates to be diligent, obtains their trust. Diligence increases the likelihood of success and success leads to confidence. Confidence leads to greater trust, which in turn forges unity and increases the strength of the organization, and so on and on. Let's see what Solomon says about diligence and how it can lead to success in all our endeavors.

"He becometh poor that dealeth with a slack hand: but the hand of the diligent maketh rich. He that gathereth in the summer is a wise son: but he that sleepeth in harvest is a son that causeth shame." Proverbs 10:4-5 [394]

"The hand of the diligent shall bear rule: but the slothful shall be under tribute." 12:24 [395]

""The slothful man does not catch his game or roast it once he kills it, but the diligent man gets precious possessions." Proverbs 12:27 [396]

"The soul of the sluggard desireth, and hath nothing: but the soul of the diligent shall be made fat." Proverbs 13:4 [397]

"The thoughts of the diligent tend only to plenteousness; but of every one that is hasty only to want." Proverbs 21:5 [398]

"[Put first things first.] Prepare your work outside and get it ready for yourself in the field; and afterward build your house and establish a home." Proverbs 25:27 [399]

Prepare, plan and act. And when you act, act with diligence and become successful.

Jackson was diligent. This was first demonstrated in his youth when he acted as constable of Lewis Country collecting debts. Years later in the military he was once heard to reflect on what he considered the right sort of man was,

"One always striving to do his duty and never satisfied if anything better can be done." [400]

This statement alone summarizes much of Proverbs and most leadership books.

Burke Davis writes that Jackson wrote in his book of Maxims,

"Disregard public opinion when it interferes with your duty.
Sacrifice your life rather than your word.
You may be whatever you resolve to be.
Lose no time; be always employed in something useful; cut off
unnecessary actions.
Be not disturbed at trifles, nor at accidents." [401]

Let nothing keep you from doing what must be done; neither doubts, nor obstacles, nor fatigue. Put others before self. Several great leaders have said, "When you help others get what they want in life, you will then get what you want."

Robertson reveals in Jackson's book of Maxims these notations,

"Industry—Lose no time; be always employed in something useful; cut off
all unnecessary actions." [402]

Colonel Sam Fulkerson said of General Thomas Jackson,

"A more fearless man never lived and he is remarkable for his industry
and energy. He is strictly temperate in his habits and sleeps very little.
Often while near the enemy, and while everybody except the guards are
asleep, he is on his horse and gone." [403]

The Reverend R. L. Dabney, Jackson's Chief of Staff for a time, shares this about his observations regarding Jackson,

One of the most marked traits of his religious character then was
conscientiousness. It ruled in every act and word; in things great, and
things minute; in his social relations and his most unrestrained remarks;
in the regulations of his appetites; in his observance of the courtesies of
life; in the disposition of his time and money.
Duty was with him the ever present and supreme sentiment. [404]

He spoke emphatically of the duty of conforming our wills to God's, and of a thoroughly cheerful acquiescence whenever his will was manifested... His favorite maxim was: "Duty is ours: consequences are God's." He spoke much also of the blessedness of a full and hearty obedience, in its effects upon the Christian's own happiness. [405]

In all three areas, our relationships with God, family, and others, we should strive to do our duty. Endeavoring to give our utmost out of devotion whether, tired, happy, or overwhelmed with life. I tell my children, "Marriage is not a fifty fifty proposition, its hundred hundred. If I endeavor to give 100% of the time without thought of what I'll receive; and if my spouse gives 100% without expecting anything in return, then we have heaven on earth. And I won't be able to give 100% much of the time perhaps, but because I try to give my all and my spouse tries to as well, we will have more success and joy in our marriage than others who do not. When we try to give all our efforts our best, then we will enjoy success in all areas of our life.

Jackson felt a man's faith and relying on God for guidance made one more successful...

"The Christian must carry his religion into everything Smith. Makes a man a better commander, a better shoemaker, a better tailor. Teaches him punctuality, fidelity,,, in the commander of an army, it calms his perplexities at a critical hour." [406]

A cadet who came to know Jackson well concluded, "He laid every plan, purpose, and desire before his Great Master, implored his direction, and when assured what the will of God was, he never deviated one hair's breadth from the path of duty." [407]

"He had long cultivated the habit of connecting the most trivial and customary acts of life with silent prayer." [408]

"His zeal and activity in the cause of religion were always among his most striking characteristics." A cadet at the time noted. "Yet while he labored constantly he did so quietly and modestly." [409]

Diligent, yet modest and humble. Conscientious, duty to what one discerned through prayer to be God's will. Yet though he demanded much of himself he was somewhat more understanding of others limitations. If we demand too much others may grow discouraged with their failures and completely quit trying. Expecting their best efforts can encourage them to give their best. Giving our best in their behalf both gives them a sense of worth, and serves as an example to inspire them.

Lieutenant colonel G. F. R. Henderson writes,

"But if he carried his conscientiousness to extremes, if he laid down stringent rules for his own governance, he neither set himself up for a model nor did he attempt to force his convictions upon others." [410]

When one has responsibility it is important that one takes this seriously. Once an organization grows a leader must train his people, giving clear guidance and direction. He or she must impart the organizations vision and mission to them. He or she must insure they possess the knowledge and skills they will need. But at some point the leader must trust them to carry out the plans decided upon. Micromanagement ruins associates and subordinates self-esteem and confidence, and inhibits trust. It also is a needless waste of the leader's time. Once he delegates responsibility based on their perceived abilities, he or she must let go and allow them to go forth and act. If they err the leader then may correct them. This process should result in their growth and the organizations strength and ability.

A leader must balance accepting the ultimate responsibility for the carrying out of plans and decisions, with giving some of that responsibility to others.

Jackson always took personal responsibility for ensuring all was well planned and acted on.

Lieutenant Moseley observed,

"The keynote of Jackson's military success - personal supervision over important tactical movements." [411]

Yet he trusted his subordinates and associates to carry out plans respecting their abilities. He balanced getting the job done with allowing others the chance to do and grow.

If he demanded the strictest compliance with his instructions, he was always content to leave their execution to the judgment of his generals; and with supreme confidence in his own capacity, he was still sensible that his juniors in rank might be just as able. His supervision was constant, but his interference rare; and it was not till some palpable mistake had been committed that he assumed direct control of his divisions or brigades. [412]

Jackson's wife said of him,

"He never appointed a man to a responsible position without knowing all about him. He would make the most minute inquiries. Was he intelligent? Was he faithful? Was he industrious? Did he get up early? This was a great point with him. If a man was wanting in any of these qualifications, he would reject him, however highly recommended. No feeling of personal partiality, no feeling of friendship, was allowed to interfere with his duty. He felt that the interests at stake were too great to be sacrificed to favoritism or friendship." [413]

It is no wonder he was so successful in the field. He became adept at attaining the correct balance between delegation and supervision. He obtained and trained the best, and then trusted them to go forth and multiply the efforts and results.

How did his men perceive him? One of his men spoke of General Jackson to his wife,

"We do not look upon him merely as our commander – do not regard him as a severe disciplinarian, as a politician, as a man seeking popularity – but as a Christian; a brave man who appreciates the condition of a common soldier; as a fatherly protector; as one who endures all hardships in common with his followers; who never commands others to face danger without putting himself in the van." [414]

Because of his ability to allow them to see his motives and dedication and caring, they saw his efforts in the proper light.

In addition to being conscientious, and balancing delegation and supervision, Jackson held nothing back when he decided on a course of action. One of the surest ways to fail at any task is to go at it half-heartedly. This can not be said of Jackson. His whole life was one of striving as a devotional says, "his utmost, for His highest."

As Robertson said of Jackson,

> *"Jackson always believed in aggressive action: prompt, fierce, and decisive. Strike the foe before he can deliver a blow. If repulsed, fall back and be ready instantly to strike again if the opportunity arises. Seek ever to change defeat into victory. If successful in the attack, pursue the enemy relentlessly and, by decisive assault, destroy the force in front. This will end the war."* [415]

To pursue the proper course of action, regardless of the cost tremendously magnifies the odds of achieving what ever you will. Research, plan, decide and then act, holding nothing back. Robertson relates the story of when his cadets were asking him about the time he manned artillery during the battle of Chapultepec. One asked why he didn't run when things grew hot.

> *"I was not ordered to do so. Had I been ordered to run, I would have done so; but I was directed to hold my position, and I had no right to abandon it."* *This resolve and devotion to duty made a strong impression on the young men.* [416]

Jackson, and on the Union's side Joshua Chamberlain, knew that when short on ammunition or hard pressed, that is when you rely on the power of giving all you've got in one last supreme effort. At the battle of Bull Run when the confederate units were being pushed back General Bee exclaimed to General Jackson,

> *"General they are driving us." Jackson replied, "Sir, we will give them the bayonet."* [417]

Often times exerting oneself and those in ones charge in one all out effort is the truest means of conserving resources as the goal is obtained faster and more completely.

> *"Better to lose one man from hard marching than five in battle."* [418]

> *"Always mystify, mislead, and surprise the enemy, if possible; and when you strike and overcome him, never let up in the pursuit as long as you have strength to follow; for an army routed, if hotly pursued, becomes panic stricken, and can then be destroyed by half their number. The other rule is, never fight against heavy odds, if by any possible maneuvering you can hurl your own force on only a part, and that the weakest part, of your enemy and crush it. Such tactics will win every time, and a small army may thus destroy a large one in detail, and repeated victory will make it invulnerable."* [419]

General George Smith Patton was very much like Jackson in his belief in these tactics. All out effort, never allowing doubts to hinder or diminish your efforts. Once you decide what needs to be done, do it or die trying.

As General Patton in World War II quoted Frederick the Great, "L'audace, L'audace, Toujours L'audace." Be audacious, ever audacious, be bold. General Patton also echoed this quote of Thomas Jackson,

"Never take counsel of your fears." [420]

Another quote of General Patton that further illustrates this is from his book, "War As I Knew It",

"Any commander who fails to obtain his objective, and who is not dead or seriously wounded, has not done his full duty." [421]

Clausewitz, another famous military man said of boldness, that it was,

" the true steel which gives the weapon its edge and brilliancy." [422]

Finally one from Basil King,

"Go at it boldly, and you'll find unexpected forces closing around you and coming to your aid." [423]

Lieutenant Colonel Henderson favors us with several similar observations in his book, "Stonewall Jackson and the American Civil war."

It by no means follows that because a man has lived his life in camp and barrack, has long experience of command, and even long experience of war, that he can apply the rules of strategy before the enemy. In the first place he may lack the character, the inflexible resolution, the broad grasp, the vivid imagination, the power of patient thought, the cool head, and, above all, the moral courage. In the second place, there are few schools where strategy may be learned, and, in any case, a long and laborious course of study is the only means of acquiring the capacity to handle armies and outwit an equal adversary. The light of common-sense alone is insufficient; nor will a few months' reading give more than a smattering of knowledge. [424]

It is no time, when the tide of victory bears him forward, for a general to take counsel of his fears." [425]

A time comes in all protracted operations when the nervous energy of the best troops becomes exhausted, when the most daring shrink from further sacrifice, when the desire of self-preservation infects the stoutest veterans, and the will of the mass opposes a tacit resistance to all further effort. "Then", says Clausewitz, "the spark in the breast of the commander must rekindle hope in the hearts of his men, and so long as he is equal to this he remains their master. When his influence ceases and his own spirit is no longer enough to revive the spirit of others, the masses, drawing him with them, sink into that lower region of animal nature which recoils from danger and knows not shame. Such are the obstacles which the brain and courage of the military commander must overcome if he is to make his name illustrious." [426]

The leader above everyone else must believe and go forth, giving his all, pulling his people and their hearts and wills into his wake, creating a tidal wave that overcomes all before it. Before closing this chapter one final point must be made. In addition to taking action diligently, one must remain sensitive to developments that occur. A good leader always observes the competition to learn from them. One has a significant advantage when one can step into the shoes of a competitor, or opponent and ask yourself, "What would I do in their place?" Then you can plan how to meet their efforts against you. Many experienced leaders such as Henderson believe that both Lee and Jackson had this ability. It has been said that Lee had it to the extent it appeared he could read his adversaries' minds. In conclusion, while procuring fresh and accurate data is crucial, and obtaining the wise advice of many good counselors vital, though developing plans and coming to decisions are necessary; if one does not act, nothing occurs. It is all for naught. One must have the courage, confidence, conviction, and faith to act. One must act decisively, with unity and the strength it conceives. Then one will achieve success, even in the face of overwhelming odds.

CHAPTER XVII.

A LEADER MANAGES HIS RESOURCES WELL – IS FISCALLY WISE

T here are many types of Resources: People, money, materials… Some of these issues we have looked at in previous chapters. Of all the resources that of people, both associates and self, is the most important. We will save it for last.

First we will look at diligence, integrity, giving to God, providing for others, and the question of debt. There are excellent books on this matter. Many famous men have related personal experiences and advice. I recommend: "Compassionate Capitalism" by Rich Devos, as well as John Avanzini's, John Sestina's and Robert Kiyosaki's books.

In reading the life of Robert E. Lee one learns that his father, Light Horse Harry Lee, a revolutionary war hero, due to bad investments became heavily in debt and served time in a debtor's prison. In addition he failed as a provider both in caring for his family and himself. He left the country and died on his return while Robert was young. This made Robert very firm in his own views on debt. Many famous men, such as Thomas Jefferson, experienced financial failure due to inability to adhere to budgets etc. So one can be a successful leader and a poor accountant and at life's end a poor man. It would seem far better to be both a successful leader, and a successful manager of one's family's funds.

When one studies the life of Jackson, one finds evidence that Thomas Jackson was diligent in all he did, and trustworthy and effective as a manager of his money. His book would tell us, be diligent in your work and you will be rewarded.

"He becometh poor that dealeth with a slack hand: but the hand of the diligent maketh rich." Proverbs 10:4 [427]

"He that gathereth in the summer is a wise son: but he that sleepeth in harvest is a son that causeth shame." Proverbs 10:5 [428]

"The thoughts of the diligent tend only to plenteousness: but of everyone that is hasty only to want." Proverbs 21:5 [429]

*"Through wisdom is a house builded; and by understanding it is established.
And by knowledge shall the chambers be filled with all precious and pleasant riches." Proverbs 24:3-4* [430]

*"Be thou diligent to know the state of thy flocks, and look well to thy herds. For riches are not forever:
and doth the crown endure to every generation?" Proverbs 27:23-24* [431]

*"He that tilleth his land shall have plenty of bread:
Be he that followeth after vain persons shall have poverty enough." Proverbs 28:19* [432]

"There is treasure to be desired and oil in the dwelling of the wise;
but a foolish man spendeth it up." Proverbs 21:20 [433]

He that loveth pleasure shall be a poor man:
He that loveth wine and oil shall not be rich." Proverbs 21:17 [434]

Being diligent in one's work, wise, and disciplined in managing the

rewards leads to financial success, and makes others more apt to trust you

in managing their affairs.

Be honest in your business dealings.

"A False balance is an abomination to the Lord:
but a just weight is his delight." Proverbs 11:1 [435]

"Divers weights (one for buying and another for selling),
and divers measures, both of them are like abomination to the Lord."
Proverbs 20:10 [436]

"It is naught, it is naught, saith the buyer:
but when he is gone his way he boasteth." Proverbs 20:14 [437]

"He that is greedy for unjust gain troubles his own household:
but he who hates bribes will live." Proverbs 15:27 [438]

"Wealth (not earned but) won in haste or unjustly or from the production
of things for vain or detrimental use (such riches) will dwindle away,
but he who gathers little by little will increase (his riches)."
Proverbs 13:11 [439]

"An inheritance may be gotten hastily (by greedy unjust means) at the
beginning: but the end thereof shall not be blessed." Proverbs 20:21 [440]

*"To have respect of persons and to show partiality is not good,
neither is it good that man should transgress for a piece of bread."
Proverbs 28:21* [441]

*"He that by usuary (charging excessive interest) and unjust gain
increaseth his substance,
he shall gather it for him that will pity the poor." Proverbs 28:8* [442]

*"He that covereth his sins shall not prosper:
but whoso confesseth and forsaketh them shall have mercy."
Proverbs 28:13* [443]

*"He who has an evil and covetous eye hastens to be rich and knows not
that want will come upon him." Proverbs 28:22* [444]

*The Lord will not suffer the soul of the righteous to famish: but he casteth
away the substance of the wicked." Proverbs 10:3* [445]

*"A faithful man shall abound with blessings:
but he that maketh hast to be rich (at any cost) shall not be innocent."
Proverbs 28:20* [446]

If you are not trustworthy in financial dealings, few will put their business, resources, and finances in your keeping, now or ever. To be honest, in all of one's dealings, pays greater and longer lasting dividends.

*"A good name is rather to be chosen than great riches,
and loving favor rather than silver and gold." Proverbs 22:1* [447]

Money should never be the be all, end all of your efforts. Don't lose your focus. Always realize that people are more important than money. Or as a friend of mine often quotes Winston Churchill, "We make a living by what we get. But we make a life by what we give." Zig Ziglar has said, "If you help enough people get everything in life they want, you'll get everything in life you want." Use your business to help build people, don't use people to help build a business.

In addition to paying one's debts in a timely manner, waiting to buy things needed until one can pay cash, saving some of what you earn, and investing some, one should put first giving money to support God's church and to helping others. J. Vernon McGee shares more nuggets of wisdom in regards to money and finances in his commentary.

"The Lord has said that if one sows sparingly, he shall also reap sparingly. That is a general principle. It certainly also applies to giving to the work of the lord. [448]

He that witholdeth corn, the people shall curse him:
but blessing shall be upon the head of him that selleth it.
Proverbs 11:26" [449]

"Riches profit not in the day of wrath:
but righteousness delivereth from death." Proverbs 11:4 [450]

"There are those who [generously] scatter abroad, and yet increase more; there are those who withhold more than is fitting or what is justly due, but it results only in want." Proverbs 11:24 [451]

Mercy, that is, generosity in caring for those less fortunate, results in a good reputation, a strong self-image, and an untroubled conscience that rewards one with peaceful sleep. Sow in generosity to others and reap a

harvest of friends, who will remember, and come to your aide in times of

personal trouble.

"Labour not to be rich: cease from thine own wisdom. Wilt thou set thine eyes upon that which is not? For riches certainly make themselves wings; they fly away as an eagle toward heaven. Proverbs 23:4-5 The whole thought here is this: There is nothing wrong in being rich. There is nothing wrong in working to be rich. However, don't make that the goal of your life. Wealth should not be the very object of our hearts. Some men have a lust, a thirst, a covetousness to make the almighty dollar, and the dollar becomes their god. A child of God is not to do that. A wealthy man told me, 'I do not make money for the sake of money. I make money for what it can do. At first I made money for what it could do for me. Now I make money for what it can do for God.'" [452]

"Better is a dry morsel, and quietness therewith, than an house full of (feasting on offered sacrifices) sacrifice with strife." Proverbs 17:1 [453]

Jackson's wife tells us of his practices in this regard...

"In his own giving for religious purposes, he adopted the Hebrew system of tithes, contributing every year one tenth of his income to the church. He was a liberal giver to all causes of benevolence and public enterprises, and during the war he gave bounteously of his means to promote the spiritual interests of the soldiers." [454]

Jackson's and Lee's favorite book has much to say on this.

"He that trusteth in his riches shall fall: but the righteous shall flourish as a branch." Proverbs 11:28 [455]

"He that despiseth his neighbor sinneth: but he that hath mercy on the poor, happy is he." Proverbs 14:21 [456]

"By humility and the fear of the Lord are riches, honor, and life."
Proverbs 22:4 [457]

"The Lord will destroy the house of the proud
but he will establish the border of the widow." Proverbs 15:25 [458]

"He that giveth to the poor shall not lack:
but he that hideth his eyes shall have many a curse." Proverbs 28:27 [459]

"He that hath a bountiful eye shall be blessed;
for he giveth of his bread to the poor." Proverbs 22:9 [460]

"He that oppresseth the poor to increase his riches, and he that giveth to
the rich, shall surely come to want." Proverbs 22:16 [461]

"Rob not the poor, because he is poor: neither oppress the afflicted in the
gate: For the Lord will plead their cause,
and spoil the soul of those that spoiled them." Proverbs 22:22-23 [462]

J. Vernon McGee, the writer of my favorite commentary says this...

"There is that maketh himself rich, yet hath nothing: there is that maketh
poor, yet hath great riches." Proverbs 13:7

Here is another example of the old nature that we all have. If we are poor
we want to put up a front, to keep up with the Jones. We pretend to have
more than we actually have. Some people drive a Cadillac automobile
simply to impress other folk, even though they can't really afford it. Some
live in neighborhood they really cannot afford." [463]

Don't spend your money in an attempt to "look good". Instead, endeavor

to "become" good and thereby attract others trust, which leads to success,

and wealth.

When budgeting set a goal, plan well to meet that goal, and then act exercising self-discipline in all areas. Make sure you have enough to meet unexpected eventualities.

When establishing a relationship with a supply corporation, ensure they are able to supply the quality needed, in the quantity you need, when you need it.

Once again on the issue of debt, do not get into debt, and if already in debt, get out as soon as possible, and stay out. As Lee advised his sons,

> *"Avoid debt, the sink of mental power and the subversion of independence."* [464]

> *"He that is surety (security) for a stranger shall smart for it: and he that hateth suretiship is sure (secure from its penalties)"* *Proverbs 11:15* [465]

> *"A man void of understanding striketh hands, and becometh surety (security) in the presence of his friend."* *Proverbs 17:18* [466]

> *"The rich ruleth over the poor, and the borrower is servant to the leader."* *Proverbs 22:7* [467]

> *"Be not thou one of them that strike hands, or of them that are sureties for debts."* *Proverbs 22:26* [468]

Make no mistake; debt makes you a slave to the creditor.

Regarding Jackson, it appears he avoided going into debt and was conscientious in this and in his duties of constable which included collecting debts,

Prompt in meeting his own engagements, he enforced the same upon others.
Collecting debts is always a thankless task, but it had to be done; and Jackson did it kindly, but firmly. [469]

Now we need to spend a little time on considering the wise use of that most important resource placed in a leaders hand, people. Staff, subordinates, associates etc., and his or her self.

<u>Know your limits,</u>

"His ambition was too great to flag, but neither man nor beast can go beyond certain limits." [470]

"...his staff was not large enough, and it was impossible for them to do the work required of them." [471]

When urged by Major Roberdeau Wheat not to expose himself unnecessarily Jackson replied, "I will try and not go into danger, unnecessarily. But Major you will be in danger greater than I, and I hope you will not get hurt. Each of us has his duty to perform, without regard to consequences; we must perform it and trust to providence." [472]

Jackson only appears to have disappointed others in his combat performance once, and that one occasion seems to have been due to lack of sufficient rest. One must as a leader accept one's limitations, and work within them whenever possible. Doing this prevents impairing one's personal productivity later. Someone told me one of the oil companies had a commercial that said, "you pay me now or you'll pay me later." This applies here as well. You rest now or you'll spend time convalescing later. I had been a work-a-holic for years. Then my physical plant failed and I developed one medical problem after another. The reason, not enough sleep. The cure, rest and then learning how to work more efficiently, to say no to less important tasks and offers, and to continue to take good care of myself, so I could be worthy of taking care of others'.

Treasure the precious resource of people, yourself, and others. As Jackson told others…

"Better to lose one man from hard marching than five in battle." [473]

"Frugality—Make no expense but to do good to others or yourself: i.e., waste nothing." [474]

When questioned about casualties I believe both Grant and Patton said something similar to the effect, "I would rather loose 1,000 men now to save 10,000 men later. Sometimes leaders must make hard decisions and sacrifice people they care about. Yet even this may at times be done out of love for the others. Sacrificing a few to save many is hard, but may be the only option.

Generals Jackson, Lee and Patton all demonstrated to their men that they valued them and took pains to avoid the loss of any one while concentrating on achieving their cause. Because of this their men respected them and loved them, being loyal even unto death. On more than one occasion when Jackson's men ran out of ammunition they fought with rocks for their commander. How can a leader fail when he or she has gained this type of loyalty from their people. Loyalty won because the leader was first loyal, the leader first, valued, loved, them. I believe it may have been General Schwarzkopf who said something to the effect that, many look at a company and see a company. A leader looks at a company and sees 100 people, 100 sons and daughters. They are precious, treat them so, value each one.

Mentor your replacement.

His men rely on him too much and I fear if he were lost his army might lose spirit." [475]

John Maxwell in one of his many excellent books on leadership stresses the importance of the leader mentoring and preparing for his own replacement. When a leader does this there are two benefits. 1) He can duplicate himself and so his efforts. I have trained seven people in my organization to do my key tasks as well as myself. Now I can achieve the same tasks in seven different locations at the same time! 2) It is possible for the leader to prolong the organization's benefits, its fruits, and obtain results not one, or five, or ten, years but that many lifetimes. If one develops a really excellent system, organization, one that contributes significantly to this world's benefit, one wants to ensure it withstands any event. If you pour your life into establishing such a corporation, why would you not want it to survive and continue beyond yourself. Therefore it is important to think on this and make preparations to replace oneself. To mentor that person or persons, who will replace you. Hopefully those people will become better than you, and will continue to grow and improve the organization. To set in place a system and training method that will teach leaders to teach leaders, on and on. I have seen two of this country's wealthiest business entrepreneurs do this. They have inspired me to begin to look at and mentor my possible replacements. Do the same. Your life is important, as are your people, your family and your mission. Don't fail to entrust them to hands as good if not better than your own. Perhaps this book and the others we have discussed can help you.

CHAPTER XVIII.
A LEADER MAINTAINS BALANCE

In the beginning of this book we discussed three pillars. We made the argument that everyone has three pillars or core priorities: God, Family, and Calling or Profession.

We have looked at Jackson's faith and how important his relationship to God was.

"To attempt to portray the life of Jackson while leaving out the religious element, would be like undertaking to describe Switzerland without making mention of the alps." Moses D. Hoge [476]

"James Power Smith, one of his faithful aides in war, observed in later years that 'the religion of Jackson was the man himself. It was not only that he was a religious man, but that he was that rare man among men to whom religion was everlasting.' Smith also made a prediction: 'The religion of Stonewall Jackson will be the chief and most effective way into the secret spring of the character and career of this strong man.' " [477]

In writing to his sister Jackson says,

"...within the past years, I have endeavored to live more nearly unto God. And now nothing earthly could induce me to return to the world again... For my part, I am willing to go hence when it shall be his great will to terminate my earthly career. ...Rather than violate the known will of God, I would forfeit my life. It may seem strange to you, but nevertheless such a resolution I have taken, and I will by it abide." [478]

In writing to his wife he says,

"If I know my unworthy self, my desire is to live entirely and unreservedly to God's glory. Pray, my darling, that I may so live." [479]

We have seen how seriously Jackson took his profession of being a soldier, his calling to serve others as a teacher for a time, and before and after as a soldier for his country. Margaret Junkin Prestin, his sister-in-law said,

"To serve his country, to do God's will, to make as short work as possible of the fearful struggle, to be ready for death if at any moment it should come to him-these were the uppermost ideals of his mind, and he would put aside, with an impatient expression, the words of confidence and praise that would be lavished on him." [480]

In fact I believe that Jackson, even as a teacher, was preparing to become a better soldier should his country ever need him to retake that role.

In this chapter I want to again look at the pillar of Family. I believe that in this life it is only too easy to become side tracked, so focused on one or two pillars that one gets out of balance and growth as a person, and in one's life as a leader, ceases and can deteriorate.

It's possible to overemphasize one's relationship with God. When I was 21 years old I had a very personal encounter with God. When you have a relationship with someone who is very significant in your life, you want to learn all about that person. You want to spend all your time in learning their likes and dislikes. You want to really get to know them. There is a tendency to do this to the point that you neglect others in your life. I had always believed I was unlovable. That I would never be loved. I believed God was a bug smasher. An omnipotent being who looked down upon us as though we were a bunch of ants. If an ant got out of line, God reached down and squashed him. Then one day I found myself in a difficult spot and no where else to turn. I told God off. I told Him, that in my opinion, He was doing a pretty poor job of running things and that I was getting cheated. I told Him I wanted just more time to prepare for an exam, didn't care about the outcome, didn't care if I flunked, I just wanted a chance, deserved a chance. I learned the next day our college had closed for three days to study the rights of black students and if our college was unfair to them. I studied three days and flunked the exam. And realized with a shock that my prayer had been answered exceedingly well. I began to think maybe this God was real, and really cared. I began talking with Him and shortly after encountered Him in a more personal way and decided He was indeed my Father, and that He loved me. I wanted to be the best son I could be. So, I began to read the Bible. It was wonderful spending time with this new found parent who really cared and I then made a mistake. I spent all my time basking in His love and reading, and neglected my family who needed my help. I became so, "heavenly minded I was no earthly good", as a friend of mine has said. My earthly father after bearing with me for many days finally pointed out to me that I was selfishly applying myself to my desires and not to helping others. I remember thinking, "Blessed are the persecuted." (I forgot the numerous times in the Bible one finds, *"Honor thy father and mother."* And how God links it with obtaining success in life.) But very soon I realized my dad had been right. I had become selfish in my seeking my own comfort, I had lost my focus, my balance, and I saw my Heavenly Father wasn't too pleased either.

"Faith without works is dead." James 2:20 [481]

Yea a man may say, Thou hast faith, and I have works: shew me thy faith without thy works, and I will shew thee my faith by my works." James 2:18 [482]

It is through our dealings with others that we encounter God, and these same encounters are the vehicle by which we do his will, serve others, and grow as his children.

In like manner we can also become so focused on our profession that we become out of balance, neglecting our families and our God. As men particularly we seem to feel that it is our role, what society expects of us, to be good breadwinners. Whether male or female it seems to be our obligation to achieve something, to grow in our chosen way of life. And so, we start out learning the tasks expected of us. We get a job, become good at it and work it hard. The harder we work the more we advance and achieve. The more income and rewards we obtain for our family. We become better as providers and achievers. At this point it is so very easy to so focus our energies, talents, and minds on this, on achieving and obtaining that suddenly it becomes everything. The means of achieving an end becomes the end in and of itself. We forget God and family, and if we don't realize what we are doing may turn around one day to find that somewhere along the path we became separated from them, perhaps forever. Too often we wake up to this after it is too late and spend the rest of our lives wondering what went wrong. Having obtained a good life, only to spend it alone and miserable. Perhaps realizing deep within ourselves, yet never admitting it, that we failed those who counted on us, our family, our God and ourselves. We chose the wrong end. We wandered off the true path. We lost our balance.

If we are to be successful in life, as family members, children of God, and as leaders in our profession, then we need to constantly look at our three pillars and the emphasis we are placing on each. We need to focus on all three. There will be times one pillar needs more attention. We need to address that and act. We need then to look again at all three and reassess if another pillar needs more attention now, or do we need to give all three our attention equally.

We have seen Jackson focused on the pillars of God and Profession. Perhaps we need to look again at how well he focused on the third pillar, family. Here are many comments he made to his wife.

"In daily walks I think much of you. I love to stroll abroad after the labors of the day are over, and indulge feelings of gratitude to God for all the sources of natural beauty with which he has adorned the earth...As my mind dwells on you, I love to give it a devotional turn, by thinking of you as a gift from our heavenly Father." [483]

"One of my greatest desires for advancement is the gratification it will give my darling, & of serving my country more effectively...I should be very ungrateful if I were not contented, and exceedingly thankful to our kind Heavenly Father." [484]

His wife tells us that,

"He luxuriated in the freedom and liberty of his home, and his buoyancy and joyousness of nature often ran into a playfulness and abandon that would have been incredible to those who saw him only when he put on his official dignity." [485]

He kept his wife ever aware of his love for her.

"Time forbids a longer letter, but it does not forbid my loving my esposita." [486]

"Always believe that your husband never forgets his little darling." [487]

As he lay dying he would look on his wife and tell her,

"My darling...you are very much loved. You are one of the most precious little wives in the world." [488]

Those who read the letters of Thomas Jackson and George S. Patton will see how these men constantly thought of their spouses and shared their lives and told them of their love for them. Reading Mary Anna Jackson's book one sees a husband who never stopped courting his spouse. It appears that Thomas Jackson did indeed see the importance of the three pillars in life and was better than most at keeping them in balance. I believe such a focus and effort is responsible in a large measure for true success in life. Success that lasts, and that inspires others.

Is there anywhere in Jackson's favorite book that we can find guidance to enable us to grow as a spouse and parent? Both Solomon and Paul have much to say on the subject.

"Whoso findeth a wife (spouse) findeth a good thing, and obtaineth favor of the Lord." Proverbs 18:22 [489]

"Let the husband render unto the wife due benevolence: and likewise also the wife unto the husband." 1 Corinthians 7:3 [490]

"Wives, submit yourselves to your husbands, as it is fit in the Lord. Husbands, love your wives and be not bitter against them." Colossians 3:17,18 [491]

"Children, obey your parents in all things: for this is well pleasing to the Lord. Father, provoke not your children to anger, lest they be discouraged." Colossians 3:20,21 [492]

"Train up a child in the way he should go: and when he is old, he shall not depart from it." Proverbs 22:6 [493]

Good parents are a blessing to their children and good children a blessing to their parents.

Some of the best commentary on this topic can be found in James Vernon McGee's Commentary on the Book of Ephesians. On page 159 he relates,

May I say to young people today: Don't accept anything that is second-rate. Don't take anything but the very best God has to offer you. "Nevertheless let every one of you in particular so love his wife even as himself; and the wife see that she reverence her husband." Ephesians 5:33 "Nevertheless" brings us down to earth with a jolt. This is the practical part about marriage. Oh how sin has marred this glorious relationship-as it has marred everything else-but this relationship can be yours if you want it to be the best. Paul brings the reader back to the ordinary routine of Christian living in the home. "Let each love his wife as himself." This shows the kind of husband to whom the wife is to be in subjection. The husband and the wife in the home are to set forth in simplicity the mystery of the coming glory. [494]

Again McGee shares on page 165,

And ye fathers, provoke not your children to wrath: but bring them up in the nurture and admonition of the Lord. "Nurture" means discipline, and "admonition" means instruction. Bring them up in the discipline and instruction of the Lord. No such commandment was given to parents under the Law. Under grace there are always mutual responsibilities and interactive duties. The parent is not to vent a bad disposition on a child or punish him in a fit of rage. It is the parents' duty to teach the child the truths of the scriptures and then to live them before the child. Don't provoke your children to wrath. As a believer you are to live at home like a believer. "Fathers" includes the mothers also. However, the emphasis, I think, is on the father because the disciplining and training of the child is actually his responsibility, but it does include the mother also. Children are not to be provoked to anger. This doesn't mean they are to be treated as if they were a cross between an orchid and a piece of Dresden china. [495]

Thomas Jackson kept all three pillars, or priorities in focus. He worked at improving in each role and he met with success that still inspires today. (It is interesting to note that one of George S. Patton's relatives was in Jackson's army. It is also interesting to note how Patton not only quoted Jackson's maxim's but also fought like Jackson and like Jackson won a great many decisive battles for his country.) Both were students at The Virginia Military Institute. And, both were students of the Bible.

A reading of Jackson's favorite book basically teaches us to cherish and revere our spouse like our own lives; to be willing to sacrifice one's life for them. It also reveals that the best thing we can do as parents is to honor and revere our spouses and not just talk the talk when it comes to Bible teachings, but to walk the walk.

When we are on our deathbed we don't want to regret that we focused too much on our profession and not enough on our family.

CHAPTER XIX.

A LEADER RESTS ON ROCK – IS CALM AMIDST THE STORM

"My religious belief teaches me to feel as safe in battle as in bed, God has fixed the time of my death. I do not concern myself about that." [496]

W hen I read of one event in Jackson's life I was struck by what I felt was the key to all his greatness as a leader. The above verse stood out from all other quotes as I realized what made all of these men so successful. I found the same thing in Lee's life and in the life of Patton and other great leaders.

"Divine love and personal self-discipline combined in Jackson to create absolute fearlessness. He could look forward to the next world because he was so constantly aware of its existence." [497]

"James Power Smith, one of his faithful aides in war, observed in later years that 'the religion of Jackson was the man himself. It was not only that he was a religious man, but that he was that rare man among men to whom religion was everlasting.' Smith also made a prediction: 'The religion of Stonewall Jackson will be the chief and most effective way into the secret spring of the character and career of this strong man.' " [498]

"A Shenandoah matron stated, 'He may well be fearless, as he is ready to meet his God; his lamp is burning, and he waits for the bridegroom.' " [499]

Robertson reveals, based on looking at Jackson's personal Bible, that Jackson's two favorite Bible verses appear to have been: Revelation 21:4 "And God shall wipe away all tears from their eyes; and there shall be no more death, neither sorrow, nor crying, neither shall there be any more pain: for the former things are passed away." However the verse that most inspired him was Romans 8:28: "And we know that all things work together for good to them that love God, to them who are the called according to his purpose." [500]

Jackson's faith, Dr White noted, "not only made him brave, but gave form, order, direction and power to his whole life." [501]

Jackson repeatedly was in combat where he was at risk of being killed. There were times those with him advised him to retire to an area where he would be less exposed and at risk. I believe the opening statement sums up why he was so at peace.

"My religious belief teaches me to feel as safe in battle as in bed, God has fixed the time of my death. I do not concern myself about that." [502]

At the battle of Chancellorsville Union General Hooker appears to have become overcome with fear, incapable of directing his troops out of fear. All after he had made excellent plans and put them into action. He did everything we have talked about necessary for a leader to succeed and then lost the opportunity when he became paralyzed with fear.

Jackson won many engagements, as did Lee, when greatly outnumbered. He was able to plan and then take enormous risks and win the victory. Why? I believe it comes down to the fact that he was able to stay calm and completely at rest. How did he, how could he, remain calm with bullets whistling about his ears? I can imagine many a Christian saying, what he said, that he was safe as in bed because of his faith in God. But many of those Christians would say it while retiring to safety behind a large rock. Jackson said it with a smile while exposed to enemy fire, and that many times has made all the difference. Because he had the faith to be calm. That allowed him to out think everyone else because he was calmer, because of his faith and trust in God.

One can argue that all his training was responsible, that his ability to place himself in his opponents shoes was responsible. But Hooker was trained and a military leader. And others had insights and ability to discern what their opponents were thinking, though in fact this was relatively rare. I have come to believe after 8 years of studying Jackson and Lee that it was their faith more than anything else that allowed them to perform better and so repeatedly win against overwhelming odds.

Their faith, and their living it, openly being an example of men of faith. Their men saw it and were inspired. Their men saw and experienced the manifestation of their faith in the love they received from these great generals. And being loved, as thought they were their children, they came to love and trust and lay down their lives for them. They came to fight with a unity and strength no one else could match.

When he and the cadets were called to go to Richmond, and all had been made ready, he sent Dr. White to pray over the young soldier. Jackson then closed the door of his bedroom and sat down with Anna, taking his Bible and reading from the fifth chapter of Second Corinthians words which deeply moved his wife: "For we know that if our earthly house of this tabernacle be dissolved, we have a building of God, a house not made with hands, eternal in the heavens." [503]

His friend Elder Lyle –one of the noblest specimens of a Christian that ever lived—used to question him very closely on his Christian experience, and one day asked him if he really believed the promise: "All things work together for good to them that love God, to them that are called according to his purpose." He said that he did, and the elder asked: "If you were to lose your health, would you believe it then?" "Yes! I think I should." "How if you were to become entirely blind?" "I should still believe it." "But suppose in addition to your loss of health and sight, you should become utterly dependent upon the cold charities of the world?" "He thought for a moment and then replied with emphasis: "If it were the will of God to place me there, he would enable me to lie there peacefully a hundred years." [504]

At first Manassas after a Union bombardment left 27 injured or dead what calmed his men was Jackson who rode back and forth along the line moving "about in that shower of death as calmly as a farmer about his farm when the season are good."...Another noted that a glance revealed, "The trust in God, and utter reliance on His will were surely there- but no apathetic calmness. The blaze of the eye was unmistakable-there plainly was a soul on fire with deep feeling, and the ardor of battle... A slumbering volcano clearly burned beneath that face so calm and collected." An aura of confidence seemed to surround him. So did Jackson's quiet words: "Steady, men, steady! All's well!" He offered those reassurances despite the fact that he had been painfully wounded. [505]

Colonel Bradley T. Johnson of the First Maryland in an engagement realized the general was praying, "Abstracted, dead to the strife, and blind to all around, his soul communed alone with his God." [506]

...it was observed that he was much in prayer, but this was his custom previous to every battle. Even upon the field he was often seen to lift his eyes and raise his right arm as if in earnest prayer, and sometimes it seemed that while his soul was thus lifted up in supplication, the Lord of hosts heard and answered, giving him the victory. [507]

Jackson was optimistic because he had faith. [508]

This chapter has a great many quotes from their favorite book, the Bible.

Read these and see if you don't have a greater sense of calm, and trust, and

a positive outlook, a true feeling, but hopefully, a true knowing, that you are

safe, that He will guide you to success.

"As the whirlwind passeth, so is the wicked no more:
but <u>the righteous is an everlasting foundation.</u>
The fear of the Lord prolongeth days:
but the years of the wicked shall be shortened.
The hope of the righteous shall be gladness:
But the expectation of the wicked shall perish.
The way of the Lord is strength to the upright:
But destruction shall be to the workers of iniquity.
<u>The righteous shall never be removed:</u>
But the wicked shall not inhabit the earth."
Proverbs 10:25,27,28,29,30 [509]

"The <u>righteous is delivered out of trouble,</u>
and the wicked cometh in his stead." Proverbs 11:8 [510]

"The wicked are overthrow and are not:
but <u>the house of the righteous shall stand."</u> Proverbs 12:7 [511]

*"The wicked is snared by the transgression of his lips:
but <u>the just shall come out of trouble."</u> Proverbs 12:13* [512]

*"<u>There shall no evil happen to the just:</u>
but the wicked shall be filled with mischief." Proverbs 12:21* [513]

*"In the way of righteousness is life;
and in the pathway thereof there is no death." Proverbs 12:28* [514]

*"<u>In the fear of the Lord is strong confidence:
and his children shall have a place of refuge."</u> Proverbs 14:26* [515]

*"The fear of the Lord is the fountain of life,
to depart from the snares of death." Proverbs 14:27* [516]

*"The Lord is far from the wicked:
but he heareth the prayer of the righteous." Proverbs 15:29* [517]

*"Commit thy works unto the Lord,
and thy thoughts shall be established." Proverbs 16:3* [518]

*"He that handleth a matter wisely shall find good:
and whoso trusteth in the Lord, happy is he." Proverbs 16:20* [519]

*"<u>The name of the Lord is a strong tower:
the righteous runneth to it and are safe."</u> Proverbs 18:10* [520]

*"The spirit of a man will sustain his infirmity;
but a wounded spirit who can bear." Proverbs 18:14* [521]

*'The fear of the Lord tendeth to life: and he that hath it shall abide
satisfied;
he shall not be visited with evil." Proverbs 19:23* [522]

*"Say not thou, I will recompense evil:
but wait on the Lord and he shall save thee." Proverbs 20:22* [523]

"The fear of man bringeth a snare:
but whoso putteth his trust in the Lord shall be safe." Proverbs 29:25 [524]

"Therefore thus saith the Lord God, Behold, I lay in Zion for a foundation
a stone, a precious corner stone, a sure foundation: he that believeth shall
not make haste (hasten away in panic)." Isaiah 28:15 [525]

"For thus saith the Lord God, the holy One of Israel; in returning and rest
shall ye be saved, in quietness and confidence shall be your hope."
Isaiah 30:15 [526]

"Blessed is the man that trusteth in the Lord, and whose hope the Lord
is." Jeremiah 17:7 [527]

The Lord is good, a strong hold in the day of trouble; and he knoweth them
that trust in him." Nahum 1:7 [528]

For the scripture saith, Whosoever believeth on him shall not ashamed (or
disappointed). Romans 10:11 [529]

"And they were helped against them, and the Hagarites were delivered
into their hand, and all that were with them:
for they cried to God in the battle, and he was entreated of them:
because they put their trust in him." 1 Chronicles 5:20 [530]

"Our fathers trusted in thee: they trusted, and thou didst deliver them."
Psalms 22:4 [531]

"The Lord is my strength and my shield; my heart trusted in him, and I am
helped: therefore my heart greatly rejoiceth:
and with my song I will praise him." Psalms 28:7 [532]

"Many sorrows shall be to the wicked:
but he that trusteth in the Lord, mercy shall compass him about(surround
him)." Psalms 32:10 [533]

"O Lord of hosts, blessed is the man that trusteth in thee."
Psalms 84:12 [534]

" The fear of man bringeth a snare:
but whoso putteth his trust in the Lord shall be safe." Psalm 29:25 [535]

Every word of God is pure: he is a shield unto them that put their trust in
him. Psalms 30:5 [536]

King David, perhaps more than any other leader, experienced trials of every kind; and turned to God and found the security and calm that makes all the difference. All of Psalm 18 speaks of this eloquently. I suggest when you experience the trials and challenges of leadership to read this. Actually do more than read it, pray it, speak it out loud and you too will find that strong arm that will uphold you, and that peace that overcomes all adversity.

Lee experienced many failures and defeats as did Jackson. Their optimistic outlook wasn't based on a false sense of being invincible. Yet for Lee, he even after the final defeat at Appomatox never felt defeated, hopeless. I believe he felt very tired and exhausted. I believe he felt disappointment. But I don't believe he ever felt defeated. And I don't believe he ever lost hope; for his hope and trust were in God. In fact he was the south's source of hope after the war. He spent his life teaching young people and setting an example for all of forgiveness and willingness to be reconciled to his former

enemies. He went about striving to be a good citizen.

He spent the remainder of his life as President of Washington College

helping educate the young to give them greater chance to succeed in this life

and in the next life.

"I shall be disappointed, sir- I shall fail in the leading object that brought me here, unless these young men become real Christians; and I wish you, and the others of your sacred profession, to do all you can to accomplish this. I dread the thought of any student going away from the college without becoming a sincere Christian." [537]

When you trust in something as big as God it is impossible to be

permanently defeated. Oh you can fail, you can lose a battle here and there,

but you will never give up, or quit. You can and will be victorious.

"God uses these times of real stress and strain and testing to develop our spiritual character. That is the way he enables us to grow. It is in the hour of trial that you and I manifest the spiritual strength that we have." [538]

Jackson repeatedly told his soldiers, 'Never take counsel of your fears.' No place for fear existed if faith were strong. [539]

In these next quotes it is as if Jackson speaks to us, personally, of how

to succeed; even when things are not perfect and all is not going as well as

hoped.

"We are all children of suffering in this world…Amid affliction let us hope for happiness…However dark the night, I am cheered with an anticipated

glorious and luminous morrow...No earthly calamity can shake my hope in the future so long as God is my friend." [540]

When wounded he was heard by Captain James Power Smith to say, "Many would regard [these injuries] as a great misfortune; I regard them as one of the blessings of my life." "All things work together for good to them that love God." Smith quoted. "Yes, that's it, that's it. [541]

"In taking a retrospective view of my own life, each year has opened... with increased promise...I too have crosses, and am at times deeply afflicted...but I am improved by the ordeal...by throwing myself upon the protection of Him whose law book is the wonderful Bible. I would not part with this book for countless universes." [542]

Recognizing the sovereignty of the Lord of Hosts, he interceded for his veterans, that "the Almighty would cover them with his feathers, and that his truth might be their shield and buckler." [543]

"What a consoling thought it is, to know that we may, with perfect confidence, commit all our friends in Jesus to the care of our Heavenly father, with an assurance that all should be well with them." [544]

"Is there not comfort in prayer, which is not elsewhere to be found?" [545]

Let us all unite more earnestly in imploring God's aid in fighting our battles for us. The thought that there are so many of God's people praying for His blessing upon the army greatly strengthens and encourages me. The Lord has answered their prayers, and my trust is in Him, that He will continue to do so. If God be for us, who can be against us? That He will still be with us and give us victory until our independence shall be established, and that He will make our nation that people who God is the Lord, is my earnest and oft-repeated prayer. While we attach so much importance to being free from temporal bondage, we must attach far more to being free from the bondage of sin." [546]

We have looked at some traits that truly successful leaders have manifested and shared with others. We have looked at the concept of attaining and maintaining balance in our lives to place us in a position to succeed and to maintain that success. We have discussed looking ahead, and preparing to continue one's work through raising up successors, mentoring them to replace us.

If we have lived a life of balance then as we go to the next life our traits learned and balanced growth will go on with us to comfort and encourage us.

Are you young, old, sick, well? How close are you to that doorway into the beyond. 50 years or 50 minutes. One of my dearest friends and business partners, a young man of nineteen left at the close of one of our business meetings one evening a year ago. "I'll see you tomorrow." We shook hands it was often hard for us to part as we enjoyed each others company so. 15 minutes later his car was smashed by a semi-truck. The next day as I held his hand while his family and loved ones waited for Dr.s to disconnect his life support machines and harvest his organs to give life to others I thought, "I had always felt it was you who would hold my hand as I died, and would comfort my family. I never thought it would be the other way around."

Less than two years before we met and decided to venture into business together. Less than a year prior to his accident he had attended an interdenominational church service with me while we were in another state for a business conference. He had gone forward and given his life to Christ.

It is a fact that no one really knows when his or her time to leave this earthly plane will come. Perhaps regardless of our current circumstance we each need to think of the future. To paraphrase The Bible, what sense does it make to spend one's entire life striving for fame and wealth that lasts but a moment, doesn't it make more sense to look at what is more lasting and really matters? What could be more important than our relationship with loved ones and God? Wouldn't it be wise to check our balance from time to time? To look at our life realistically and make any corrections needed before it is too late. To come to the right decision for us, so we too can have that outlook like Thomas Jackson.

"Nothing earthly can mar my happiness. I know that heaven is in store for me; and I should rejoice in the prospect of going there tomorrow…I have as much to love here as any man, and life is very bright to me. But still I am ready to leave it any day, without trepidation or regret, for that heaven which I know awaits me, through the mercy of my Heavenly Father. And I would not agree to the slightest diminution of one shade of my glory there- no, not for all the fame I have acquired or shall ever win in this world." [547]

Wouldn't it be best to always be prepared for whatever life may bring?

As my father said, "Live each day as though you would live forever, but

also live each day as though it were your last." To be ready in case this day

is your last.

Several times after he had been shot, it had flashed on the general that he might be dying. Each time, will had rallied him. Now he felt sure his end had come and he committed himself into the hands of his maker. A sense of peace at once possessed him. Calm and exaltation of spirit followed. There, helpless on the ground, he felt he had won the victory of faith in conflict with Death. [548]

"The wicked is driven away in his wickedness:
but the righteous hath hope in his death." Proverbs 14:32 [549]

CHAPTER XX.
CONCLUSION

I have studied leadership for around forty years. I have been in leadership positions for nearly 30 years. When I studied the lives of Robert E. Lee and Thomas J. Jackson, they taught me so much. Much of that time I was being pressured to be less than ethical. I found myself among people who had ceased to have ideals and dreams, who believed it was impossible to be ethical. I believe God gave me three friends to help me through these times. To help me stay the course and hold to my ideals, to be ethical, and to lead as a servant leader, for that truly is what a leader is, a servant to his or her people. He gave me George S. Patton, Robert E. Lee and Stonewall Jackson. They have become dear friends, mentors, and brothers.

One or two years ago I was struck by the fact that Jackson so freely, openly, sincerely, lived his faith. His relationship with God was so visible, because he never dreamt of hiding it. That is why I feel he is such a tremendous example to us today. I wrote this book because I believe that the Bible and the lives of great leaders have much to teach us today. Proverbs was written by a successful leader who took his lessons from another who I believe was an even greater ruler, though not as wealthy and known, King David. Psalms is perhaps even greater than Proverbs as a leadership book.

I recently reflected on David. When Samuel was looking to anoint one of Jesse's son's as God had instructed him to. He arranged a feast and had Jesse bring his sons. As each one came in Samuel looked at them. Each was tall and handsome and as each one came in Samuel thought, "This one must be the one." He picked every one but David. The rest were all good looking, taller, more polished. David at last was brought in from tending the sheep, it seems even his family had forgotten about him. He was short and no doubt his hair was blown into a bad hair-do, his cheeks wind burned, his skin dry. He had been spending his time out with his sheep, that was his duty, he was a Sheppard. He was out caring for his sheep, defending those entrusted to his care from attacks by lions and bears. His family had even forgotten he was out there, they forgot to ask him to come to the feast. Perhaps they assumed he didn't matter. Surely David couldn't be needed at the feast.

Yet when Israel and the Philistines were arrayed in battle. When the champion of the Philistines strutted out every day and challenged Israel to sent out a man to fight him, everyone hid in the lines, no one was eager to go out and fight him. David comes into camp and hears Goliath and gets mad. Goliath is treating his country and Lord with disrespect. He learns that for the one who dares to take the risk there is wealth, marriage into the king's family, and freedom from paying taxes. Much like the opportunities found in starting one's own business, in free enterprise here in the United States. The chance of greater wealth and tax breaks, and associating with other visionaries.

David's tall handsome, talented brothers, hold back, they aren't willing to take the risk. And, they talk disparagingly to David, telling him he's just a nothing and a glory seeker. His family do everything they can to discourage him. David decides to follow his own path, he trusts in his God and seeks to do His will. He walks out and look at the fight. Goliath is big, and heavily armored, with a gigantic weapon. Sort of like a big tank. But David is small, mobile, and has a sling that means he doesn't have to get close to have an effect. David is more like a fighter plane/tank buster. David walks with God. David wins hands down. Knocks out Goliath, cuts off his head and is victorious.

Often it isn't the good looking, good smelling, multi-degreed, popular, politically-correct, trendy, cover person who makes the great leader, in fact in my experience it never is. It is the underdog type, ethical, honest, frank, humble, kind, servant who believes in what he or she is doing, who strives to do God's will, that changes the course of the world.

In conclusion I'd like to share some comments from James Vernon McGee's commentary on Proverbs. Then I'd like to present the core traits we've looked at again, as a more concise list to guide your path as a leader.

"The child of God needs to be fortified. He needs to get into the strong tower. He needs to be in his strong city and have the high wall around him. What is it? Well, it is a knowledge of the Word of God. We need to recognize that we are living in very difficult times and we are being tested. Oh, how important is a knowledge of the word of God. ...There is no substitute for digging into the Word of God. If you don't understand it, read it again. If you don't understand it the second time, go over it once more. Then if you don't understand it the third time through, there is something wrong, and you need to go to the Lord and tell him you're not getting it. Ask him to help you. The Spirit of God is our teacher. I know I am telling you this accurately because he hasn't yet let me down in this matter of understanding His Word." [550]

"I noticed this little motto...
'Joy is like the flag that is flown in the heart when the master is in residence.' I like that. When the Lord Jesus Christ becomes first choice in your life, when he has top priority, then you will not have that broken spirit that we hear so much about today. Give God the first choice. Give of your time, your effort, your thoughts, your companionship, and your money, and see what happens." [551]

A man that hath friends must shew himself friendly: and there is a friend that sticketh closer than a brother. Proverbs 18:24 [552]

"God gave Israel definite rules regarding their markers: 'Thou shalt not remove thy neighbors landmark, which they of old time have set in thine inheritance, which thou shalt inherit in the land that the Lord thy God giveth thee to possess it.' Deuteronomy 19:14. These markers went for generation to generation and were very important. When a man got old and feeble and his eyesight began to fail him, his neighbor might want to slip over and move the marker a couple of feet to increase his parcel of land. God said that kind of thing was forbidden. It would be totally dishonest of course. Now I am going to make a spiritual application of this. You may think I am square when I say this, but I believe that today we have seen the landmarks of the Christian faith removed. They have been removed by what was at first called modernism, and is now called liberalism....Now I want to say this" Instead of moving forward and removing landmarks, we need to start moving backward to get back many of the ancient landmarks. Those ancient landmarks made this nation great. The landmarks of moral values, the spiritual truths, the biblical basis- all have been removed....I say that we need to get back to the old landmarks which our nation had at the beginning. [553]

" 'See thou a man diligent in his business? He shall stand before kings; he shall not stand before mean men." Proverbs 22:29' God says that He intends to reward the diligent man. You remember that the Lord Jesus said that in eternity his commendation would be: '...Well done, thou good and faithful servant...' Matthew 25:21. His commendation will not be based on the amount of work you have done, or on the number of people to whom you have witnessed, or on how hard you have worked, but on how faithful you have been to the task he has given you." [554]

Thank you for taking this journey with me. I wish you God's blessings and balance.

Proverbs Success Traits

Seek wisdom and understanding. Apply your heart to wisdom and your ears to understanding. In every gain get wisdom. Understand that the study of the Bible reveals much about human nature, about how to succeed in business, and about how to live a successful life. If you want wisdom, pray, ask God to reveal it, read and listen. The commandment is a lamp for your way, teaching a light, and reproofs of discipline a way of living to keep you safe.

Accept discipline and reproof. They teach major lessons quickly. Listen to advice. Wisdom is with those who take advice. In an abundance of counselors is plenty. Every plan is best confirmed by counsel. In every endeavor, in peace and in war, wise counsel should be sought. Listen to knowledgeable people, then use discernment to make your decision.

Discretion will protect you, discernment will guard you. In all you do be observant; and be discerning in speaking with others and especially in choosing those you will listen to.

<u>Choose partners and people who are faithful, trustworthy, and reliable</u>.

<u>Plan well, develop skills of observation and insight</u>. Look ahead. Count the costs. Take a straight course. Be prudent, look ahead, be observant, see dangers and avoid them.

<u>Be not wise in your own eyes, trust in God</u>. In all you do give Him the credit and He will guide you. Seek His will and you will learn it. Don't become hurt and discouraged when things go wrong, realize that it is in the trials and defeats that we learn and grow the most.

<u>Be reverent</u>. Know deep down, that it is He that gave you life, that gave you your talents, and who sees and believes in your potential. Acknowledge that it is He who will make or break you. Give Him the credit, the honor, and the glory before self and others. Reverence for God leads to confidence, prosperity, a long life, and security for your children. Put Him before self. Trust Him completely.

<u>Be humble</u>. Humility leads to grace and honor. Humility and reverence lead to riches, honor, health, and long life. Don't put your self forward. Don't seek a better place or position. Let your works cause others to elevate you. Don't seek your own glory, don't praise yourself. Always remind yourself that it is God who has accomplished it. Remember Paul's advice, He uses the weak and foolish and achieves great things through them, so that others see that it is He who did it, and what He can do through them. It is better to be humble and sit with the poor, than to share riches with the proud.

<u>Confess and forsake your sins</u>. Know your weaknesses. Seek someone to be accountable to so that you don't ignore areas you need to improve in. So that you may spotlight the areas you are not proud of. When you look on them with open eyes, and admit the problems, then you can with His help work to correct them. Work with God to change.

<u>Choose your company carefully and set proper goals</u>. Not goals for personal wealth, but goals to serve others. Do not toil to get wealth, surrender that personal ambition for the love of others. Don't desire socializing with

the rich. Avoid alcohol, excesses in diet, and getting into debt for any reason, but especially avoid it if to impress others. Avoid the selfish. Don't hunger after ill-gotten gains. Don't worry or be anxious. Avoid jealousy. Hate covetousness. And you will live longer and healthier. Serve others. Trust in God.

Always have a kind word for others. Your words should be pleasant and ease other's burdens. Your words should be used to comfort and gladden others. The words of the righteous heal, and turn away anger. Your words should impart good sound counsel and that which will help them grow. Be merciful, not arrogant. Remember God's forgiveness of your faults. Be kind, and seek to do good. Be patient always, avoid rashness and haste. Control your tongue and your temper. Deal considerately with others. Avoid strife. Seek to understand. Practice justice and loving-kindness. Don't speak ill of others. Don't spread rumors. If you can't say anything positive, don't speak. Never judge another.

Forgive and be merciful. Forgive seven times seventy times.

<u>Control your mouth</u>. He who guard his mouth controls himself. He who cannot comes to ruin. Be pure.

<u>Be diligent in your work</u>. In work is profit. Dream, develop a vision, set goals, see them, speak what you want. He who tills the ground will have his bread, but he who follows vain pursuits lacks sense. Wealth gathered in haste dwindles away. He who gains by labor increases. Know the condition of your business, keep your mind on those you serve, clients, associates, subordinates. Those who focus on their work and others, and strive to do what is right, will have plenty for years to come. Those who focus on leisure will starve.

<u>Remember with the fruit of his words a man is well satisfied</u>. Truthful lips endure forever. You will get what you speak. The tongue of the wise heals, a soothing tongue is a tree of life. A good word at the right time is greatly appreciated. Good news refreshes others. Do not boost, Do not exaggerate. Do not flatter. Don't speak ill of another. Say only what will be of benefit to others. Resolve not to open your mouth to speak, unless you have first thought about it, and can speak without passion that which

will bless another.

Control your temper. The prudent person restrains anger. A wise person ignores an insult. One slow to anger quiets contention. He who covers an offense seeks love. Don't bring up that which alienates others. Never reveal the secrets of another. Be a peace maker.

Do not borrow, do not get in debt. He who hates debt is secure. He who trusts in riches will fail. Do not get into debt, pay cash for everything, if in debt get out as quickly as possible and avoid it in the future.

Don't lend, don't overcharge. Better a little righteousness by fair means, than a large income without justice.

Roll your work over onto God. Trust in Him, don't rely on yourself. Don't be proud. In all you do acknowledge God, and He will direct all your paths. When a person's ways please God, he makes even their enemies be at peace with them.

Tithe and be faithful. When you are paid, immediately give 10% to God's work. Give another 10% to help others. Invest, save, another 10%. Be creative with these blessings He gives you. He gives you all you have as a steward. Be a good and faithful servant. Expect blessings.

Be at peace. Do good. Focus on the positive. Do not fret, do not worry, do not be anxious, trust him and have health, wealth, and peace.

A true leader has no boss but God. A leader is not the served, they are the servant. Remember, keep your balance. In addition to keeping your focus on the three areas understand this, they are also your three great strengths and supports. God, Family, and Others, support systems that will get you through all things. Your family might at times fail but your team and God won't. There may be times your team might fail you, but not your family and God. And through the toughest times God, well, He'll never fail you. Turn to God, accept His love and that of your family, and your team. Associate with other leaders always, leaders like David, and like you.

May God talk to your heart and mind and soul. May He help you be the leader you want so to be, and an even greater leader, the one He wants you to be.

I'm excited about your success. Let me know how you're doing. I hope we meet on the journey.

BIBLIOGRAPHY

The Bible, King James Version.

The Amplified Bible1987; Zondervan, Grand Rapids.

Baehr, Ted and Wales, Susan.   Faith in God and Generals.   2003; Broadman & Holman Publishers, Nashville.

Dabney, R.L. Life and campaigns of Lt. General T.J. (Stonewall) Jackson. 1983; Sprinkle Publications, Harrisonburg.

Davis, Burke. They Called Him Stonewall. 1954; Buford Books Inc. Short Hills.

Douglas, Henry Kyd. I Rode With Stonewall. 1940; University of North Caroline Press.

Freeman, Douglas southall. Lee's Lieutenants, Vol 1 and 2. 1942;

Touchstone, New York.

Glatthaar, Joseph T. Partners In Command. 1994; The Free Press, New York.

Harrison, Shorne. Stonewall: Memories From The Ranks. 1998; Signal Tree Productions, Rockbridge Baths.

Henderson, G.F.R. Stonewall Jackson and The American Civil War. 1994; Smithmark Publishers Inc., New York.

Jackson, Mary Anna. Life and Letters of "Stonewall" Jackson by His Wife. 1995; Sprinkle Publications, Harrisonburg.

Jones, J. William. Christ in the Camp. 1986; Sprinkle Publications, Harrisonburg.

Lee, Robert E. Recollections and Letters of General Robert E. Lee. 1904; Konecky & Konecky, New York.

McGee, James Vernon. Thru The Bible Commentary Series: Proverbs.

1991; Thomas Nelson Publishers, Nashville.

Patton, George S. War As I Knew It. 1995; Houghton-Mifflin Company,

Boston.

Robertson, James I. Jr. Stonewall Jackson The Man, The Soldier, The

Legend. 1997; Macmillan Publishing Inc., New York.

Robertson, James I. Jr. Stonewall Jackson's Book of Maxims. 2002;

Cumberland House, Nashville

Tanner, Robert G. Stonewall in The Valley. 1996; Stackpole books,

Mechanicsburg.

Tate, Allen. Stonewall Jackson, The Good Soldier. 1956; J.S. Saunders

and co., Nashville.

Wilkins, J. Steven. Call of Duty. 1997; Highland Books, Elkton.

END NOTES

Introduction

1. Burke Davis, They Called Him Stonewall (Short Hills: Buford Books, 1999) 110.

2. Davis 118.

3. Davis 123-124.

4. Kings James Version of The Bible, Ephesians 5:25

5. Davis 133.

6. J. Steven Wilkins, Call of Duty (Highland Books, 1997) 190.

7. Wilkins 191.

8. Davis 110.

Chapter I.

9. James I. Roberston Jr., Stonewall Jackson The Man, The Soldier, The Legend (Macmillan, 1997) xii.

10. Robertson (1997) 35.

11. Davis 63.

12. Roberston (1997) 190.

13. Roberston (1997) 190.

14. Davis 83-84.

15. Roberston (1997) 135.

16. Roberston (1997) 100.

17. KJV Proverbs 2:2

18. KJV Proverbs 2:3-6

19. KJV Proverbs 4:7

20. KJV Proverbs 13:10

21. KJV Proverbs 23:12

Chapter II.

22. KJV Proverbs 11:14

23. Marcus Aurelius, Meditations of Marcus Aurelius, Translator ASL Farquarson, (Oxford, 1944) 48.

24. John C. Maxwell, Living at The Next Level (Thomas Nelson, 1996) 58.

25. KJV Proverbs 6:23.

26. KJV Proverbs 12:1.

27. KJV Proverbs 12:15.

28. KJV Proverbs 13:1.

29. KJV Proverbs 13:10.

30. KJV Proverbs 13:18.

31. KJV Proverbs 13:20.

32. KJV Proverbs 15:8.

33. KJV Proverbs 15:22.

34. KJV Proverbs 15:31.

35. KJV Proverbs 15:32.

36. Davis 50-51.

37. Robertson (1997) 124.

38. Robertson (1997) 137.

39. Robertson (1997) 148.

40. Robertson (1997) 154.

41. Davis 87.

42. KJV Proverbs.

43. KJV Proverbs.

44. KJV Proverbs.

Chapter III.

45.   James I. Robertson Jr.   Stonewall Jackson's Book of Maxims (Cumberland House, 2002) 29.

46. Robertson (2002) 30.

47. Robertson (2002) 31.

48. KJV Proverbs 27:17.

49. Davis 441.

50. Robertson (1997) 291.

51. Mary Anna Jackson, Life and Letters of Stonewall Jackson, (Sprinkle, 1995) 209.

52. Robertson (2002) 46.

53. KJV Proverbs 13:17.

54. KJV Proverbs 20:18.

55. Robertson (1997) 19.

56. Robertson (1997) 541.

57. Robertson (1997) 91.

58. Robertson (1997) 435.

59. Shorne Harrison, Stonewall: Memories from The Ranks.(Signal Tree, 1998) 7.

60. KJV Proverbs 12:23.

61. KJV Proverbs 13:3.

Chapter IV.

62. Robertston (1997) xii.

63. Robertson (1997) 35.

64. Jackson 111.

65. Robertson (1997) 35.

66. Davis 55.

67. Davis 83.

68. Davis 54.

Chapter IV.

69. Robertson (1997) 135.

70. Robertson (2002) 14.

71. Davis 125.

72. Robertson (1997) 621.

73. Robertson (1997) 447-448.

74. G.F.R. Henderson, Stonewall Jackson And The American Civil War. (Smithmark, 1994) 186.

75. Jackson 81.

76. Henderson 41.

77. Robertson (2002) 77.

78. Henderson 196.

79. Harrison 19.

Chapter V.

80. Robertson (1997) xii.

81. Robertson (1997) xii.

82. Robertson (1997) 134.

83. KJV Psalm 146:5

84. Robertson (1997) 137.

85. Robertson (1997) 85.

86. Jackson 287.

87. Douglas Southall Freeman, Lee's Lieutenants, Vol 2. (Touchstone,1942) 567.

88. Robertson (1997) 428.

89. Robertson (1997) 449.

90. Jackson 332.

91. KJV Proverbs 3:5-6.

92. Robertson (1997) 683.

Chapter V.

93. Freeman 47.

94. Freeman 66.

95. KJV Psalm 146:3.

96. KJV Psalm 118:8-9.

97. Freeman 500.

98. KJV Psalm 146:3.

99. KJV Psalm 20:7 .

100. KJV Psalm 37:5.

101. KJV Psalm 40:4.

102. KJV Psalm 44:6.

103. KJV Psalm 55:23.

104. KJV Psalm 56: 3-4.

105. KJV Psalm 115:11

106. R. L. Dabney, Life and Campaigns of Lt. General T.J. (Stonewall) Jackson. (Sprinkle, 1983) 121

107. KJV Psalm 146:5

108. Dabney 110.

109. Jackson 324.

110. Jackson 326.

111. KJV Psalm 62:6-8

112. Jackson 124.

113. Jackson 124.

114. KJV Isaiah 26:4

115. Jackson 370.

116. Davis 55.

117. Robertson (1997) 697.

118. KJV Proverbs 3:5-6.

Chapter V.

119. Davis 67.

120. Jackson 363.

121. Robertson (1997) 525.

122. KJV Isaiah 12:2.

123. KJV Isaiah 30:15.

124. KJV Psalm 125:1.

Chapter VI.

125. Robertson (1997) 134.

126. KJV Psalm 33:8.

127. KJV Psalm 33:18-19.

128. KJV Proverbs 1:7.

129. KJV Proverbs 9:10.

130. KJV Proverbs 22:4.

131. KJV Deuteronomy 8:6.

132. KJV Proverbs 1:7.

133. Dabney 87.

134. Robertson (1997) 135.

135. Robertson (2002) 88.

136. Dabney 653-654.

137. Robertson (1997) 135.

138. Robertson (1997) 209.

139. Robertson (1997) 137.

140. Robertson (1997) 135.

141. Robertson (1997) 181.

142. Robertson (1997) 252.

143. Dabney 320.

144. Robertson (1997) 444.

145. Robertson (1997) 482.

146. Robertson (1997) 516.

147. Dabney 110

148. Rev. J. William Jones, Christ in The Camp. (Sprinkle,1986) 110.

149. Harrison 7.

150. KJV Matthew 20:25-28.

Chapter VII.

151. Harrison 30.

152. KVJ Samuel 22:28.

153. KVJ Psalm 18:27.

154. KJV James 4:6

155. KJV Psalm 25:9

156. KJV Psalm 147:6

157. KJV Isaiah 66:2.

158. KJV Proverbs 11:2.

159. KJV Proverbs 15:33.

160. KJV Proverbs 18:12.

161. KJV Proverbs 22:4.

162. Robertson (1997) xv.

163. Robertson (1997) xv.

164. Robertson (1997) 180.

165. Robertson (1997) 428

166. Robertson (1997) 449.

167. Robertson (1997) 277.

Chapter VIII.

168. Jackson 332.

169. Davis 157.

170. Jackson 370.

171. Robertson (1997) 126-127.

172. Robertson (1997) 183.

173. Dabney 251.

174. Robertson (1997) 582.

175. Jackson 384.

176. Jackson 406-407.

177. Robertson (1997) 636.

178. Robertson (1997) 681.

179. Dabney 490.

180. Jackson 120.

181. Harrison 30-31.

182. Robertson (1997) 685.

183. Harrison 44.

184. Harrison 43.

185. Harrison 41.

186. Harrison 41.

187. Harrison 58.

188. Freeman 561.

189. Henderson Vol 2 196

190. Amplified Bible Matthew 20:26.

Chapter VIII.

191. KJV Proverbs 3:7.

192. KVJ Psalms 3:11-12.

193. KJV Psalms 6:23.

194. KJV Proverbs 12:15.

195. KJV Proverbs 13:10.

196. Amplified Proverbs 13:10.

197. KJV Proverbs 13:16.

198. KJV Proverbs 13:18.

199. KJV Proverbs 15:31-32.

200. KJV Proverbs 19:20.

201. KJV Proverbs 28:13.

202. Robertson (1997) 137.

203. Davis 128.

Chapter IX.

204. KJV Proverbs 1:20-22.

205. Robertson (2002) 88.

206. Robertson (2002) 90.

207. KJV Proverbs 14:15.

208. KJV Proverbs 4:11-12.

209. KJV Proverbs 16:3

210. KJV Proverbs 22:3.

211. KJV Proverbs 24:27.

212. KJV Proverbs 4:26-27.

213. KJV Proverbs 15:21.

214. Robertson (1997) xv.

215. Robertson (1997) 91.

216. Robertson (1997) 100.

217. Robertson (1997) 209.

218. Robertson (1997) 457.

219. Harrison 36.

220. Freeman 688.

221. Davis 94.

222. Jones 90.

223. Jackson 459.

224. KVJ Matthew 16:26

Chapter X.

225. Robertson (2002) 79.

226. Robertson (2002) 79.

227. Robertson (2002) 79.

228. Robertson (2002) 79-80.

229. Jackson 204.

230. Jackson 209.

231. Henderson 61.

232. Henderson 376.

233. Dabney 105.

234. Robertson (1997) 66.

235. Henderson 62.

236. KJV Proverbs 12:10.

237. KJV Proverbs 29:7.

238. KJV Proverbs 29:14.

239. KJV Exodus 22:22

240. Isaiah 1:17.

241. Jeremiah 21:3

242. KJV Psalm 37:28.

243. KJV Proverbs 3:33.

244. KJV Proverbs 10:24.

245. KJV Proverbs 10:30.

246. KJV Proverbs 11:4.

247. KJV Proverbs 11:5.

248. KJV Proverbs 13:21.

249. KJV Proverbs 16:8.

250. KJV Proverbs 21:3.

251. KJV Proverbs 21:15.

252. KJV Proverbs 21:21.

253. KJV Proverbs 28:21.

254. KJV Psalm 106:3.

255. KJV Psalm 5:12

256. KJV Psalm 11:7.

257. KJV Psalm 37:25.

258. KJV Psalm 64:10

259. KJV Psalm 72:7.

260. KJV Psalm 112:4.

261. KJV Proverbs 3:12.

262. KJV Proverbs 6:23.

263. KJV Proverbs 13:24.

264. Wilkins 314.

265. George S. Patton War As I Knew It.

266. Patton.

267. Patton

268. Patton

Chapter XI.

269. Wilkins 269.

270. KJV Matthew 18:21-22.

271. KJV Luke 7:47.

272. KJV Psalm 32: 1,3.

273. KJV Ephesians 4:32.

274. Robertson (1997)

275. Robertson (2002) 64

276. Ted Baehr and Susan Wales, Faith in God and Generals. (Broadman and Holman, 2003) 6.

277. Amplified Acts 5:31

Chapter XII.

278.   Dictionary of The English Language, College Edition, Laurence Urdang Ed. (Random House, 1968) 692.

279. KJV Titus 2:7.

280. KJV 1 Kings 9:4-5.

281. 1 Chronicles 29:17.

282. KJV Psalm 78:70-72.

283. KJV Proverbs 10:9.

284. KJV Proverbs 11:3.

285. KJV Proverbs 13:6

286. Robertson (1997) 35

287. Harrison 30.

288. Robertson (1997) 91.

289. Robertson (1997) 540.

290. Dabney 653-654.

291. Jackson 409.

292. Harrison 58.

293. Dabney 716.

Chpater XIII

294. Amplified Proverbs 15:4.

295. KJV Proverbs 15:13

296. KJV Proverbs 10:21

297. KJV Proverbs 16:21.

298. Robertson (1997) xv.

299. Jackson 57.

300. Robertson (1997) 135.

301. Robertson (1997) 623.

302. Robertson (1997) 139.

303. Freeman 2.

304. Amplified 1 Corinthians 10:10.

305. Freeman 643.

306. Jackson 124.

307. Jackson 124.

308. Jackson 376.

309. Jackson 408.

Chapter XIV.

310. KJV Proverbs 16:32.

311. KJV Proverbs 21:23.

312. KJV Proverbs 17:28.

313. KJV Proverbs 1:5.

314. KJV Proverbs 12:15.

315. KJV Proverbs 17:27.

316. KJV Proverbs 22:17.

317. Robertson (2002) 112.

318. Robertson (2002) 42.

319. KJV Proverbs 18:13.

320. KJV Proverbs 18:4.

321. KJV Proverbs 18:6-8.

322. KJV Proverbs 18:21

323. KJV Proverbs 19: 5,9.

324. KJV Proverbs 21:23.

325. KJV James 3:2-10.

326. KJV James 3:13.

327. KJV Proverbs 12:18.

328. KJV Proverbs 18:7.

329. KJV Proverbs 18:8.

330. KJV Proverbs 18:19.

331. KJV Proverbs 29:20.

332. KJV Proverbs 10:17.

333. KJV Proverbs 15:1.

334. KJV Proverbs 19:11.

335. KJV Proverbs 20:3.

336. Robertson (2002) 104.

337. KJV Proverbs 29:11,20.

338. Harrison 33.

339. Robertson (2002) 64.

340. KJV Proverbs 12:23.

341. KJV Proverbs 13:3.

342. KJV Proverbs 15:2.

343. KJV Proverbs 18:7.

344. KJV Proverbs 25:9.

345. Davis 194.

346. KJV Proverbs 10:21.

347. KJV Proverbs 16:24.

248. Robertson (1997) 263.

349. Harrison 88.

350. KJV Proverbs 20:15.

351. Jackson 124.

352. Robertson (1997) 697.

353. KJV Proverbs 12:19,22.

354. KJV Proverbs 19:5,9.

355. KJV 2 Corinthians 1:4.

356. Freeman 561.

357. KJV Proverbs 12:25.

358. KJV Proverbs 15:13.

359. Davis 347.

Chapter XV.

360. KJV 2 Chronicles 10:7.

361. KJV Proverbs 28:18.

362. KJV Proverbs 3:3-4.

363. KJV Proverbs 3:27-28.

364. KJV Proverbs 14:22.

365. James Vernon McGee, Through The Bible-Proverbs. (Thomas nelson,

1991) 35.

266. KJV Proverbs 12:10

367. KJV Proverbs 11:17.

368. KJV Proverbs 14:21.

369. KJV Proverbs 20:28.

370. KJV Proverbs 19:17.

371. KJV Proverbs 22:9.

372. KJV Proverbs 15:15.

373. KJV Proverbs 15:17.

374. Jackson 108.

375. Robertson (1997) 183.

376. Dabney 121.

377. Robertson (1997) 577.

378. Henry Kyd Douglas, I Rode With Stonewall. (University of North Carolina, 1940) 102.

379. KJV Proverbs 27:5-6.

380. Robertson (2002) 46.

381. Robertson (2002) 66.

382. KJV Proverbs 27:17.

383. 27:21.

384. KJV Proverbs 19:22.

385. KJV John 10:11.

386. Robertson (1997) 685.

387. Harrison 58.

388. Wilkins 267.

389. Wilkins 279.

390. Wilkins 268.

391. Wilkins 280.

392. Robert E. Lee, Recollections and Letters of General Robert E. Lee. (Konecky & Konecky, 1904) 49.

393. Lee 138.

Chapter XVI.

394. KJV Proverbs 10:4-5.

395. KJV Proverbs 12:24.

396. Amplified Proverbs 12:27.

397. KJV Proverbs 13:4.

398. Proverbs 21:5.

399. Proverbs 25:27.

400. Robertson (1997) 541.

401. Davis 94.

402. Robertson (2002) 77.

403. Robertson (1997) 451.

404. Dabney 87.

405. Dabney 653-654.

406. Davis 441.

407. Robertson 137.

408. Henderson 61.

409. Robertson (1997) 180.

410. Henderson 62.

411. Harrison 133.

412. Henderson 376.

413. Jackson 209.

414. Jackson 204.

415. Robertson (1997) xiv.

416. Robertson (1997) 182.

417. Robertson (1997) 264.

418. Robertson (1997) 422.

419. Robertson (1997) 447-448.

420. Robertson (1997) 451.

421. Patton

422. Carl von Clausewitz, On War. (Penguin, 1982)

423. Norman Vincent Peale, You Can If You Think You Can. (Fawcett, 1974)

424. Henderson 409.

425. Henderson Vol 2 41.

426. Henderson Vol 2 196.

Chapter XVII

427. KJV Proverbs 10:4.

428. KJV Proverbs 10:5.

429. KJV Proverbs 21:5.

430. KJV Proverbs 24:3-4.

431. KJV Proverbs 27:23-24

432. KJV Proverbs 28:19.

433. KJV Proverbs 21:20.

434. KJV Proverbs 21:17.

435. KJV Proverbs 11:1

436. KJV Proverbs 20:10.

437. KJV Proverbs 20:14.

438. Amplified Proverbs 15:27.

439. KJV Proverbs 13:11.

440. KJV Proverbs 20:21.

441. Amplified Proverbs 28:21.

442. KJV Proverbs 28:8.

443. KJV Proverbs 28:13.

444. Amplified Proverbs 28:22.

445. KJV Proverbs 10:3.

446. KJV Proverbs 28:20.

447. KJV Proverbs 22:1.

448. McGee 108.

449. KJV Proverbs 11:26.

450. KJV Proverbs 11:4.

451. KJV Proverbs 11:24.

452. McGee 195.

453. KJV Proverbs 17:1.

454. Jackson 63.

455. KJV Proverbs 11:28

456. KJV Proverbs 14:21.

457. KJV Proverbs 22:4.

458. KJV Proverbs 15:25.

459. KJV Proverbs 28:27.

460. KJV Proverbs 22:9.

461. KJV Proverbs 22:16.

462. KJV Proverbs 22:22-23.

463. McGee 120.

464. Wilkins 37.

465. KJV Proverbs 11:15.

466. KJV Proverbs 17:18.

467. KJV Proverbs 22:7.

468. KJV Proverbs 22:26.

469. Jackson 28.

470. Robertson (1997) 498.

471. Douglas 101.

472. Douglas 103.

473. Robertson (1997) 422.

474. Robertson (2002) 474.

475. Robertson (1997) 525.

Chapter XVIII.

476. Robertson (1997) x.

477. Robertson (1997) xii.

478. Robertson (1997) 91.

479. Jackson 376.

480. Robertson (1997) xvi.

481. KJV James 2:20.

482. KJV James 2:18.

483. Davis 123-124.

484. Robertson (1997) 251.

485. Robertson (1997) 191.

486. Robertson (1997) 412.

487. Robertson (1997) 423.

488. Freeman 673.

489. KJV Proverbs 18:2.

490. KJV 1 Corinthians 7:3.

491. KJV Colossians 3:17,18.

492. KJV Colossians 3:20,21.

493. KJV Proverbs 22:6.

494. McGee 159.

495. McGee 165.

Chapter XIX

496. Davis 13.

497. Robertson (1997) x.

498. Robertson (1997) xii.

499. Robertson (1997) xvii.

500. Robertson (1997) 135.

501. Robertson (1997) 136.

502. Davis 13.

503. Davis 134.

504. Jones 90.

505. Robertson (1997) 263.

506. Robertson (1997) 482.

507. Jackson 324.

508. Robertson (1997) 623.

509. KJV Proverbs 10:25,27,28,29,30.

510. KJV Proverbs 11:8.

511. KJV Proverbs 12:7.

512. KJV Proverbs 12:13.

513. KJV Proverbs 12:21.

514. KJV Proverbs 12:28.

515. KJV Proverbs 14:26.

516. KJV Proverbs 14:27.

517. KJV Proverbs 15:29.

518. KJV Proverbs 16:3.

519. KJV Proverbs 16:20.

520. KJV Proverbs 18:10.

521. KJV Proverbs 18:14.

522. KJV Proverbs 19:23.

523. KJV Proverbs 20:22.

524. KJV Proverbs 29:25.

525. KJV Isaiah 28:15.

526. KJV Isaiah 30:15.

527. Jeremiah 17:7.

528. KJV Nahum 1:7.

529. KJV Romans 10:11.

530. KJV 1 Chronicles 5:20.

531. KJV Psalms 22:4.

532. KJV Psalms 28:7.

533. KJV Psalms 32:10.

534. KJV Psalms 84:12.

535. KJV Psalms 29:25.

536. KJV Psalms 30:5.

537. Wilkins 159.

538. McGee 204.

539. Robertson (1997) xv.

540. Robertson (1997) 139.

541. Freeman 643.

542. Davis 118.

543. Dabney 110.

544. Dabney 121.

545. Dabney 122.

546. Jackson 326.

547. Freeman 522.

548. Freeman 575.

549. KJV Proverbs 14:32

Chapter XX.

550. McGee 159-160.

551. McGee 160.

552. KJV Proverbs 18:24.

553. McGee 192-193.

554. McGee 193.

About The Author

20 Time-tested traits of leaders that will make YOU the leader you've always wanted to be!

Want to be a leader that truly makes a difference? From Solomon to Schwartzkopf you'll see the same principles repeated over and over. You'll find these 20 time-tested traits all you need to succeed as a leader be it corporate, church, volunteer, or military.

Finding yourself in the frying pan, and feel as though you're about to go into the fire? Get what you need to survive and excel in, "Leadership in The Heat of Battle."

Discover that the true leader:

- Constantly strives to grow

- Seeks mentors and utilizes every source of improvement

- Sees correction as a major growth catalyst

- Becomes who he or she associates with

- Plans well charting a course for success

- Takes action with confidence

- Sinks his or her trust in bedrock

- Knows where success comes from and gives the credit where its due

- Sets and maintains priorities

- Is just and impartial

- Has integrity and does what is right

- Knows and employs the power of positive talk

- Communicates for success

- Knows how to build trust and maximize rewards

- Manages all their resources well

- Maintains balance to avoid missing the boat

- Rests on rock, and wins victories

Assailed by doubts? Unhappy with your life? Take this book and start your journey to happiness and true success today. Get right. Know your leadership will live beyond you. Know your leadership is right. Attain the peace that comes from knowing you are leading in a way you can be proud of, and that you can lead your team to success even in the heat of battle.

Patrick B. Gillen, former Major USAF, has been in leadership positions for over 30 years. President of Intervarsity Christian Fellowship at an Ohio University and President of the student body of one of the largest nursing schools in a major city, he learned that to be a true leader means being the servant of all. Company Grade Officer of the Year at His flying squadron, Officer in charge of one of the most successful clinics in the United States Air Force, Consultant to numerous corporations through the United States saving them hundreds of thousands of dollars, CEO of three corporations, he has faced the pressures of whether to yield to what is politically correct, or to do what's right. To be a leader who cares for his people, or be a nobody who is politically correct for a paycheck. To be a leader who uses business to make people, as opposed to one who uses people to make business. Now he shares what he has learned through 40 years of studying the world's greatest, most successful, leaders.